SERMON IN A SENTENCE

St. Francis de Sales

SERMON IN A SENTENCE

*A Treasury of Quotations
on the Spiritual Life*

FROM THE WRITINGS OF

ST. FRANCIS DE SALES

DOCTOR OF THE CHURCH

*Arranged according to the Virtues of
the Holy Rosary
and Other Spiritual Topics*

Selected and Arranged by
JOHN P. McCLERNON

IGNATIUS PRESS   SAN FRANCISCO

Cover art by Christopher J. Pelicano
Cover design by Roxanne Mei Lum

Frontispiece by John R. Herried

© 2003 Ignatius Press, San Francisco
All rights reserved
ISBN-0-89870-974-1
Library of Congress Control Number 2002115583
Printed in the United States of America ∞

The same Everlasting Father who cares for you today will take care of you tomorrow and every day of your life. Either He will shield you from suffering, or He will give you unfailing strength to bear it. Be at peace then, and put aside all anxious thoughts.

—St. Francis de Sales

DEDICATION

This work is dedicated to my wonderful and supportive wife, Mary, and to the fruit of our marriage, the five beautiful children with whom God has blessed us: Christopher, Clare, Catherine, David, and Stephen.

Special thanks to my mother, Judy McClernon, whose advice and assistance in sorting through and selecting these "spiritual gems" from St. Francis de Sales have been so helpful.

My good friend Stan Twardy is also to be thanked for his able guidance and assistance. In all respects he is a true credit to his profession.

Last, but certainly not least, I wish to thank St. Francis de Sales for leaving behind such a great spiritual legacy with these treasured writings. Four centuries have not tarnished the power and grace that flowed from his pen. The "gentleman saint" still today sets hearts on fire for Jesus Christ and His Church. It is St. Francis who is really the author of this book. It is a privilege to be an instrument in bringing his advice and teachings to souls.

CONTENTS

Preface	11
Introduction	13
Acknowledgments	15
Abbreviations	19
Life of St. Francis de Sales	21

ROSARY VIRTUES

The Joyful Mysteries

1. The Annunciation of Our Lord: *Humility* 29
2. The Visitation of Elizabeth: *Love of Neighbor* 35
3. The Birth of Jesus: *Spirit of Poverty* 41
4. The Presentation in the Temple: *Obedience* 47
5. The Finding of the Child Jesus in the Temple: *Piety* 52

The Sorrowful Mysteries

1. The Agony of Jesus in the Garden: *Sorrow for Sin* 61
2. The Scourging at the Pillar: *Purity* 68
3. The Crowning with Thorns: *Courage* 75
4. The Carrying of the Cross: *Patience* 81
5. The Crucifixion: *Self-Denial* 88

The Glorious Mysteries

1. The Resurrection of Jesus from the Dead: *Faith* 97
2. The Ascension of Jesus into Heaven: *Hope* 104
3. The Descent of the Holy Spirit: *Love of God* 110

4. The Assumption of Mary into Heaven:
   Desire for Heaven — 117
5. The Crowning of Mary Queen of Heaven
   and Earth: *Devotion to Mary* — 123

OTHER TOPICS

Prayer	133
The Eucharist	141
Confession	147
The Mass	151
The Church	154
Marriage and Family Life	160
The Priesthood	166
The Bible	168
The Saints	170
The Angels	174

PREFACE

In my youth, while I was being brought up in a "Salesian Parish", I wondered why the sons of St. John Bosco were called Salesians and not "Bosconians" or Bosco Fathers. One day, one of the Fathers, to encourage my spiritual growth, put in my hands a book to read slowly and meditate upon. That was my answer! The book was the *Philothea*, or *Treatise on the Love of God*, by St. Francis de Sales.

Maturing in that Salesian environment, observing and comparing, I could see how the spirit of this magnificent, pleasant, and powerful saint was reflected in the life and demeanor of these people, children of St. John Bosco, and eventually I understood why their founder named the Congregation as he did.

As the years went by, after graduating from college with an engineering degree in metallurgy, I fell for that environment: yes, I became a Salesian! It was almost fifty years ago. Transferred to the United States to initiate a technical school in Los Angeles, I kept referring back to my old favorite readings, those by St. Francis de Sales and St. John Bosco.

Besides reading the writings of these two giants of practical and authentic spirituality, we used to hear homilies and sermons loaded with anecdotic references to their lives and their sayings, so that our world and imaginations were saturated with their spirit.

I am sad to say that the rich tradition of referring to the lives of the Saints has today all but vanished, leaving behind a vacuum that increasingly impoverishes us and the young. When I saw the work of John McClernon, I leaped with joy. I have been one of the people responsible for neglecting these "stars" among the masses of Christ's followers, depriving the faithful of valid and nourishing food for growth in holiness, which is the process of imitating Jesus and His authentic disciples.

Well, as I thumbed and read through the pages of this book I thanked God and John for making it possible and easy to remedy the negligence of my past. Hoping that, besides priests and preachers, many lay people will take advantage of this great and needed work in spreading the Kingdom, I wish with all my heart success and blessing to the author of this apostolic work.

Father Paul Maria Caporali, S.D.B. (Salesian)
Rosemead, California

INTRODUCTION

Many Catholics would like nothing better than to read the actual writings of the Church's spiritual giants. But how many do? The culture of today leads us to embrace such busy life-styles. All too often the time needed to feed the soul takes a back seat, and we end up spiritually starved. *Sermon in a Sentence* is designed for just such persons.

Imagine spending a few minutes with St. Francis de Sales, a Doctor of the Church and considered one of her greatest bishops and spiritual directors. More than four centuries have passed, and his writings and advice are still popular and effective for souls seeking the devout life and a sure road to personal sanctity. He is a master of the spiritual life, a timeless beacon of authentic Catholic spirituality for all peoples and cultures. St. Francis de Sales did it all. Servant of the poor and neglected, priest among priests, undaunted missionary, shepherd of souls, and defender of the Church. These are but a few of the titles one could attribute to this great saint. This book has been designed to bring the inspiration of his words to you in a very simple and direct format.

Hundreds of short quotations taken from the writings and sayings of St. Francis de Sales have been classified by the Christian virtues of which they speak and then arranged to complement the fifteen-decade rosary, proceeding from the first joyful mystery (the Annunciation, with its virtue of humility) to the fifth glorious mystery (the Crowning of Mary, with its virtue of devotion to Mary). For those who choose to use these excerpts for meditation while reciting the rosary, we have placed a type ornament after the tenth one, to mark the end of a decade. Additional quotations follow, for use with a rosary or for separate meditation. A selection of quotations on other spiritual topics of interest follows, bringing the reader a sample of St. Francis' insights into such subjects as prayer, the Eucharist, the Church, and family life.

It is hoped that this little book will serve as an effective introduction to one of our world's greatest spiritual masters. May these quotes and short sayings find a place in your heart and soul and draw you closer to Our Lord Jesus Christ, whom St. Francis de Sales loved and served so well.

ACKNOWLEDGMENTS

The author gratefully acknowledges permissions granted to reprint from the following sources:

St. Francis de Sales. *Introduction to the Devout Life*. Translated and edited by John K. Ryan. New York: Image Books, Doubleday, a division of Bantam Doubleday Dell Publishing Group, Inc. First published in 1972. This Image edition published 1989. © 1950, 1952, 1966 by John K. Ryan.

—— *Introduction to the Devout Life*. A new translation. London: Rivingtons, 1876. Available at www.ccel.org/d/desales/devout_life/devout_life.html. This version used by permission of Christian Classics Ethereal Library.

—— *The Sermons of St. Francis de Sales on Prayer*. Volume 1. Translated by Nuns of the Visitation. Edited by Father Lewis S. Fiorelli, O.S.F.S. Rockford, Ill.: TAN Books and Publishers, 1985. © 1985 by The Visitation Monastery of Frederick, Md., Inc.

—— *The Sermons of St. Francis de Sales on Our Lady*. Volume 2. Translated by Nuns of the Visitation. Edited by Father Lewis S. Fiorelli, O.S.F.S. Rockford, Ill.: TAN Books and Publishers, 1985. © 1985 by The Visitation Monastery of Frederick, Md., Inc.

—— *The Sermons of St. Francis de Sales on Lent, Given in the Year 1622*. Volume 3. Translated by Nuns of the Visitation. Edited by Father Lewis S. Fiorelli, O.S.F.S. Rockford, Ill.: TAN Books and Publishers, 1987. © 1987 by The Visitation Monastery of Frederick, Md., Inc.

—— *The Sermons of St. Francis de Sales on Advent and Christmas*. Volume 4. Translated by Nuns of the Visitation. Edited by Father Lewis S. Fiorelli, O.S.F.S. Rockford, Ill.: TAN Books and Publishers, 1987. © 1987 by The Visitation Monastery of Frederick, Md., Inc.

—— *Thy Will Be Done: Letters to Persons in the World*. Translated by the Very Reverend Henry Benedict Mackey. Originally published 1894 by Burns and Oates, Ltd., New York, Cincinnati, Chicago: Benziger Brothers. This edition published 1995 by Sophia Institute Press, Manchester, N.H., with extensive editorial revisions and improvements in the translation. © 1995 Sophia Institute Press.

—— *Treatise on the Love of God*. Volume 1. Translated with an introduction and notes by Rt. Rev. John K. Ryan. Rockford, Ill: TAN Books and Publishers, 1975. Originally published 1963 by Doubleday & Company, Inc., New York. © 1974 by John K. Ryan.

Blanche Jennings Thompson. *St. Francis de Sales*. A Vision Book. New York: Farrar, Straus & Giroux, 1965.© 1965 by Blanche Jennings Thompson. Used by permission of Farrar, Straus & Giroux.

The Voice of the Saints: Counsels from the Saints to Bring Comfort and Guidance in Daily Living. Selected and arranged by Francis W. Johnston. Rockford, Ill.: TAN Books and Publishers, 1986. First published and copyright 1965 by Burns and Oates, Ltd., London. © 1965, Burns & Oates. Reprinted by permission of The Continuum International Publishing Group, New York, and TAN Books and Publishers.

Scripture quotations have been taken from the following editions of the Holy Bible:

The Holy Bible, containing the Old and New Testaments. Revised Standard Version. Catholic Edition. Old Testament © 1952; Apocrypha © 1957; New Testament © 1946, 1971; Catholic Edition © 1966, by the Division of Christian Education of the National Council of the Churches of Christ in the United States of America. All rights reserved. Used by permission.

The Jerusalem Bible. Garden City, N.Y.: Doubleday and Company, Inc., © 1966 by Darton, Longman and Todd, Ltd., and Doubleday, a division of Random House, Inc. Reprinted by Permission.

ABBREVIATIONS

I1 *Introduction to the Devout Life*, by St. Francis de Sales. Translated and edited by John K. Ryan. New York: Image Books, Doubleday, 1989.

I2 *Introduction to the Devout Life*, by St. Francis de Sales. London: Rivingstons, 1876. Version used is available at www.ccel.org/d/desales/devout_life/devout_life.html.

L *Thy Will Be Done: Letters to Persons in the World*, by St. Francis de Sales. Translated by Henry Benedict Mackey. Manchester, N.H.: Sophia Institute Press, 1995.

S1 *Sermons of St. Francis de Sales on Prayer*. Volume 1. Translated by Nuns of the Visitation. Edited by Lewis S. Fiorelli, O.S.F.S. Rockford, Ill.: TAN Books and Publishers, 1985.

S2 *Sermons of St. Francis de Sales on Our Lady*. Volume 2. Translated by Nuns of the Visitation. Edited by Lewis S. Fiorelli, O.S.F.S. Rockford, Ill.: TAN Books and Publishers, 1985.

S3 *Sermons of St. Francis de Sales on Lent: Given in the Year 1622*. Volume 3. Translated by Nuns of the Visitation. Edited by Lewis S. Fiorelli,

	O.S.F.S. Rockford, Ill.: TAN Books and Publishers, 1987.
S4	*Sermons of St. Francis de Sales on Advent and Christmas*. Volume 4. Translated by Nuns of the Visitation. Edited by Lewis S. Fiorelli, O.S.F.S. Rockford, Ill.: TAN Books and Publishers, 1987.
SFS	*St. Francis de Sales*, by Blanche Jennings Thompson. New York: Vision Books, 1965.
T	*Treatise on the Love of God*, by St. Francis de Sales. Volume 1. Translated by John K. Ryan. Rockford, Ill.: TAN Books and Publishers, 1975.
V	*Voice of the Saints*. Edited by Francis W. Johnston. Rockford, Ill.: TAN Books and Publishers, 1993.

St. Francis de Sales

(1567–1622)

Doctor of the Church

Bishop and Patron of Writers and the Catholic Press

We are all born to be saints. God wills nothing less than our personal holiness. The lofty goal of personal sanctity is not the private domain of devout monks and nuns (as was the prevailing thought at the time of Francis) but is very much possible and obtainable for all people, regardless of the circumstances of their vocation and state of life. Up until the sixteenth century no one wrote about or lived this message more than St. Francis de Sales, the great French priest, missionary, and bishop. He was a champion of the common man and woman—and considered the spiritual direction of the lay people of his diocese to be his primary calling and duty as a bishop of the Church. The bishop he succeeded was truly prophetic about the young Francis when he stated, "This young man will be a great personage some day! He will become a pillar of the Church and my successor in this see." As the years unfolded all this came to be.

Francis was born in Swiss Savoy in 1567, the oldest of thirteen children in the distinguished de Sales family. His father was an aristocrat who had served his country well, and he planned for Francis to follow in his footsteps.

As a youth Francis was obedient, truthful, and very generous to those less fortunate than he. Francis was destined to be a true and loyal son of the Church and at the age of nine had already privately decided that the consecrated religious life was his calling. Books and knowledge were always his passion, and his father saw that Francis was provided with the best of educations, one suited to the French nobility of that time. At fourteen he was sent to Paris, the intellectual center of Europe. The young Francis resolved to attend the Jesuit College of Clermont, renowned for both piety and scholarship. During his six years in Paris Francis' heart became more and more set on dedicating himself to God, and he privately took a vow of perpetual chastity, placing himself under the special protection of the Blessed Mother. To please his father Francis also took lessons in riding, fencing, and dancing, but he cared little for these in practice. His formal education continued in Padua, where his father sent Francis to study law. Here, as in Paris, he was renowned for his scholarship and virtue.

At the age of twenty-four Francis returned to the de Sales estate with a doctorate in law and to a father who planned an ambitious secular career for him. Francis, however, continually frustrated his father's well-intentioned plans, including that for a well-connected marriage and a senate seat offered to Francis by the prince of Savoy. Patience was certainly a hallmark of Francis. He waited on God to make clear to him whether the desire of his heart to serve in the priesthood was His perfect will. One day while Francis was riding horseback God did make His will known to the young nobleman. Francis fell from his horse three times on this particular day, and each time his sword and scabbard fell to the ground and made the sign of a cross. That same day Francis was offered a post as provost of the bishop's cathedral canons. With his reluctant father's blessing, Francis entered the priesthood.

Francis took up his religious duties with the heart and passion of a saint, ministering lovingly to the poor, particularly devoting himself to their needs in the confessional. His simple style of preaching had a remarkable effect on all. When the bishop of Geneva begged for missionaries to evangelize the Calvinist stronghold of Chablis, Francis boldly requested to undertake this difficult and dangerous task. Facing possible martyrdom, with little or no support, he and a fellow canon embarked to bring the people of Chablis back to the Church.

The first few years were seemingly unsuccessful, marked by harassing and hostile crowds, humiliations, and few conversions. On two occasions it took the miraculous protection of God to save his life from would-be assassins who had sworn to kill the young missionary priest. But Francis' remarkable patience and confidence in God eventually won the cause. Adults, although attracted to his sermons and holiness, were afraid to come to him. But their children were not. They flocked to the missionary priest, whose kindness and gentle spirit charmed even the most hardened of hearts. The saint would later write: "You will catch more flies with a spoonful of honey than with a barrelful of vinegar."

St. Francis was always searching for new and better ways to reach the hearts of the people. And so it was that he began personally to write out by hand leaflets setting forth leading dogmas of the Church, leaving thousands and thousands of them on the doorsteps of the Chablis people. This eventually proved quite successful, and his untiring efforts using these religious tracts (he was the first to do so) and saintly demeanor led to widespread conversions. By the time St. Francis left the Chablis region, nearly all the 60,000 people had returned to the Catholic Church. His unfailing tenderness and generosity in receiving sinners and apostates back to the Church brought criticism from certain circles, but he simply replied "Has not our Blessed Lord shed His blood for them, and shall I refuse them my tears? These wolves will be changed into lambs; a day will come when, cleansed of their sins, they will be more precious in the sight of God than we are. If Saul had been cast off, we should never have had St. Paul."

The valiant and courageous efforts of this missionary priest, along with his brilliant preaching and shepherding of souls, caught the attention of Church officials. The bishop had long considered proposing Francis as his coadjutor and successor, but Francis had up to this time declined the honor, considering himself unworthy. He eventually agreed to the position, and at the death of the bishop in 1602 Francis was appointed to replace him as bishop of Geneva. In his post as bishop, the saint continued to lead a life of evangelical poverty and fulfilled his episcopal duties with characteristic zeal and devotion. Francis still preached and heard confessions, and the people flocked to his sermons. As in Chablis, children loved Francis and followed him about, anxious for his blessing. Many souls sought his advice for spiritual direction, and he was untiring in his efforts to respond faithfully to them. Over time this would lead to an immense and continuous writing campaign. Some of these saintly friends included St. Vincent de Paul and St. Philip Neri.

St. Francis' most notable association was with St. Jane de Chantal. In 1604 he noticed her listening attentively to one of his sermons and recognized her as a woman he had previously seen in a dream. She was on a path to mystical union with God and wanted Francis to provide spiritual direction. The two would became quick friends and work together for over sixteen years. God used this holy collaboration to lead both souls to great heights of spiritual perfection. Some of St. Francis' best spiritual insights and advice are contained in his many letters to this great woman, destined to be canonized herself in 1767. The two of them eventually founded the "Order of the Visitation" in 1610, a new religious order begun to meet the needs of widows and abandoned women in poor health.

The last twelve years of St. Francis' life would be the most demanding and consuming, as his health gradually failed under the ever-increasing duties placed upon him. He was truly a pastor of pastors and considered spiritual direction of souls his primary task as bishop. With this in mind, our saint wrote his famous *Introduction to the Devout Life*, one of the great spiritual classics of all time. Published in 1608, it was intended to give practical spiritual advice for lay people seeking holiness in their ordinary lives. Francis proved with his own life that one could grow in holiness even though engaged in the most active of occupations and responsibilities. He would write "A true stedfast soul may live in the world untainted by worldly breath, finding a well-spring of holy piety amid the bitter waves of society, and hovering amid the flames of earthly lusts without singeing the wings of its devout life."

The book was an instant success. St. Francis would later follow this work with another classic, *Treatise on the*

Love of God, which likewise made him famous all over Europe. Exhausted and worn out after years of continuous preaching and service to innumerable souls, St. Francis died on December 28, 1622. To quote this great saint and servant of God's people, "To love our neighbor in charity is to love God in man." His entrance into heaven was miraculously revealed to St. Jane de Chantal and many other friends and relatives.

St. Francis' body was found miraculously preserved in 1632, ten years after his death. He was beatified by Pope Alexander VII in 1661 and canonized by him four years later. Pope Pius IX conferred upon St. Francis de Sales the illustrious title of "Doctor of the Church" in 1877. St. John Bosco, inspired by the holy life of the great saint, would later found an order whose members were called Salesians after the saintly Doctor. Pope Pius XI in 1922 designated St. Francis as Patron of Journalists and Writers. The Church honors St. Francis' feast day every year on January 24.

"The whole world is not worth one soul."
—**St. Francis de Sales**

THE
JOYFUL
MYSTERIES

The First Joyful Mystery

The Annunciation of Our Lord

Humility

Whoever humbles himself like this child, he is the greatest in the kingdom of heaven.—Matthew 18:4

Humility is true knowledge. (I1 139)

If after all your efforts you cannot succeed, you could not please our Lord more than by sacrificing to Him your will, and remaining in tranquility, humility, and devotion, entirely conformed and submissive to His divine will and good pleasure. (L 3)

Consider how uncertain is the day of your death. My soul, one day you will leave this body. When will it be?... Only one thing is certain: we will die and sooner than we think. (I1 60)

The King of Glory does not reward His servants according to the dignity of their office, but according to the humility and love with which they have exercised it. (I2 135)

If we conduct ourselves with humility and good faith... God will raise us up to heights that are truly great. (I1 128)

A man who can own pearls does not bother about shells, and those who aspire to virtue do not trouble themselves over honors. (I1 134)

Humility drives away Satan and keeps the graces and gifts of the Holy Spirit safe within us. For this reason all the saints, and particularly the King of Saints and His Mother, have always honored and cherished this precious virtue. (I1 132)

If you want to know whether a man is really wise, learned, generous or noble, see if his life is moulded by humility, modesty and submission. If so, his gifts are genuine. (I2 144)

If [God] permits [our reputation] to be taken away from us, it will either be to give us a better one or to make us profit by holy humility, of which a single ounce is preferable to a thousand pounds of honor. (I1 145)

What we do for others always seems very great, but what is done for us seems nothing at all. (I1 216)

Let us make our way through these low valleys of the humble and little virtues. We shall see in them the roses amid the thorns, charity that shows its beauty among interior and exterior afflictions, the lilies of purity. (L 38)

We must suffer our imperfection in order to have perfection. I say suffer, not love or pet; humility feeds on this suffering. (L 170)

Humility consists in not esteeming ourselves above other men, and in not seeking to be esteemed above them. (I2 358)

In the end, we are really only what we are before almighty God. (SFS 79)

The more you say, the less people remember. (SFS 136)

Little deeds that proceed from charity please God and have their place among meritorious acts. (T 166)

Divine mercy renders all things useful to us; it puts all things to our advantage; it puts to our profit all our tasks, no matter how lowly and weak they may be. (T 168)

Who is sure of keeping this sacred love on the voyage of this mortal life, when so many persons of such incomparable rank on earth and in heaven have had such cruel shipwreck? (T 201)

We have received all things from God, and especially the supernatural blessings of holy love. If we have received them, why do we take glory for them? (T 215)

As a general rule, we shall do well to receive all such graces and favours humbly, making much of them, not for their own importance, but rather because it is God's Hand which fills our hearts with them. (I2 331)

It is a better state of mind to distrust our own power of resistance to temptation than to consider ourselves as sufficiently strong and safe.... We must take care that what we do not expect from our strength, we do expect from the grace of God. (L 218)

If we reflect on what we did when God was not with us, we will easily perceive that what we do when He is with us is not the result of our own efforts.... Glorify God because He alone is its author. (I1 135)

When humility and meekness are good and true they preserve us from the inflamation and swelling that injuries usually cause in our hearts. (I1 146)

Do not forget your distaff and your spindle: thread the string of little virtues, lower yourself to exercises of charity. He who says otherwise is mistaken. (L 31)

Gentleness and courtesy are incomparably more honorable than violence and pride. (SFS 166)

If you have not humility, you have not charity, and if you are without charity you are also without humility. It is almost impossible to have charity without being humble and to be humble without having charity. (S3 5)

The humble soul is always withdrawn within herself, without seeking any glory or praise for her actions.... She keeps her intention hidden, being content that God sees and knows what she does. (S3 9)

Certainly all virtues are very dear to God, but humility pleases Him above all the others, and it seems that He can refuse it nothing. (S3 49)

Prayer can rise to Heaven.... It rises there through the descent of humility. (S1 10)

The virtue of humility touches and attracts the Heart of God more than all the others. (S2 54)

Our Lord so cherished humility that He preferred to die rather than abandon its practice.... For in dying He made the most excellent and most supreme act of humility that could ever be imagined. (S2 87)

True humility...seeks not only to conceal other virtues, but above all it seeks and desires to conceal itself. (I2 149)

Obedience is a consecration of the heart, chastity of the body, and poverty of all worldly goods to the Love and Service of God. These are the three members of the Spiritual Cross, and all three must be raised upon the fourth, which is humility. (I2 176)

The Second Joyful Mystery

The Visitation of Elizabeth

Love of Neighbor

You shall love your neighbor as yourself.
—Mark 12:31

To be good [you] must have charity, and to be devout, in addition to charity [you] must have great ardor and readiness in performing charitable actions. (I1 40)

[We must] have tenderness toward our neighbors, bearing with their imperfections. (I1 127)

You must not only be devout, and love devotion, but you must make it lovable to everyone. Well, you will render it lovable if you render it useful and agreeable. (L 46)

Generally speaking, to ignore and despise an injury or calumny is a far more effectual remedy than resentment, fighting, and revenge. (I1 143)

I was hungry and you gave me to eat; I was cold and you clothed me; come, possess the kingdom prepared for you from the foundation of the world." He who is King of the poor and of kings will say this at His great judgment. (I1 166)

You must not give up or neglect friendships that nature or earlier duties oblige you to cultivate with parents, kindred, benefactors, neighbors and others. (I1 175)

It is either a weak or a sinful friendship that watches our friend perish without helping him, that sees him die of an abscess and does not dare to save his life by opening it with the lance of correction. (I1 183)

It is wonderful how attractive a gentle, pleasant manner is, and how much it wins hearts. (I2 231)

A little courtesy, a small virtue—but the mark of a true greatness. (L 31)

Every man has enough on which he ought to judge himself without taking it upon him to judge his neighbor. (I1 197)

❧

[We ought] always to judge our neighbour as charitably as may be; and if his actions are many-sided, we should accept the best. (I2 239)

Love of Neighbor

We are forbidden not to doubt but to judge. (I1 200)

The body is poisoned through the mouth, even so is the heart through the ear.... And even if we do mean no harm, the Evil One means a great deal, and he will use those idle words as a sharp weapon against some neighbour's heart. (I2 232)

After having prayed to love God, we must always pray to love our neighbor, and especially those to whom our will is not attracted. (L 45)

The man who could free the world of slander would free it of a large share of its sins and iniquity. (I1 201)

Whenever I speak of my neighbor, the tongue in my mouth is like a scalpel in the hand of a surgeon who wishes to cut between the nerves and the tendons. The stroke I give must be neither more nor less than the truth. (I1 205)

Bring souls to love God [by] infusing good inspirations into their hearts. (I1 215)

When you hear anyone spoken ill of, make the accusation doubtful if you can do so justly. If you cannot, excuse the intention of the accused party. If that cannot be done, express sympathy for him [and] change the subject of conversation. (I1 205)

Perform big, important works according to your vocation. But never forget...[to] practice those little, humble virtues which grow like flowers at the foot of the cross: helping the poor, visiting the sick, and taking care of your family. (I1 215)

You will catch more flies with a spoonful of honey than with a barrelful of vinegar. (SFS 134)

Since charity is an active quality, it cannot exist for long without either acting or dying....Charity urges the heart to which it is espoused to make it fertile with good works, for otherwise it will die. (T 206)

Truly it is a blessed thing to love on earth as we hope to love in Heaven, and to begin that friendship here which is to endure for ever there. (I2 202)

If your affections are warm and tender, your judgment will not be harsh; if they are loving, your judgment will be the same. (I2 238)

The sin of rash judgment is truly spiritual jaundice and causes all things to appear evil to the eyes of those infected with it. (I1 199)

Spare as much as possible the person to whom the vice belongs, all the more so because the goodness of God is so great that a single moment is sufficient for entreating

Love of Neighbor

His grace. And who can be sure that the one who yesterday was a sinner, and evil, will be so today? (L 81)

We must do well and in a holy and loving way what we owe to everyone, although it may be against the grain and without relish. (L 54)

Examine your heart often to see if it is such toward your neighbor as you would like his to be toward you were you in his place. This is the touchstone of true reason. (II 217)

He delighted in dealing with the poor and being with them. He always favored them. More often than not He was found among them. (S4 109)

God always greatly favors those who practice charity toward their neighbor; indeed, there is nothing that draws down His mercy upon us more abundantly....After that of the love of God, there is none greater. (S3 54)

Bearing the image of God in ourselves, all of us are consequently the image of each other. Together we constitute the image of one portrait, that of God. (S3 88)

Ought we not to love dearly the neighbor, who truly represents to us the sacred Person of our Master? And is this not one of the most powerful motives we could have for loving each other with an ardently burning love? (S3 92)

Father, forgive them." With this prayer He wanted to make us understand the love He bore us, undiminished by any suffering, and to teach us how our heart should be toward our neighbor. (S3 189)

Do you love God perfectly? Then you love the neighbor perfectly. In the measure that one of these loves increases, the other also increases. Likewise, if one diminishes, the other will soon grow less. (S2 73)

We must not be satisfied with speaking well, but we must adjust our deeds to our proposals and our works to our words if we want to be pleasing to Him. (S2 84)

Humility and charity have only one object, God, as they tend toward union with Him; nevertheless they pass from God to the neighbor, and it is in this transfer that they attain their perfection. (S2 157)

Justification, which is the effect of charity, is augmented by good works, and, it must be noted, by good works without exception. (T 167)

To love our neighbor in charity is to love God in man. (V 26)

It is to those who have the most need of us that we ought to show our love more especially. (V 28)

The Third Joyful Mystery

The Birth of Jesus

☙

Spirit of Poverty

Blessed are the poor in spirit, for theirs is the kingdom of heaven.—Matthew 5:3

By rich in spirit I mean him whose riches engross his mind, or whose mind is buried in his riches. He is poor in spirit whose heart is not filled with the love of riches, whose mind is not set upon them. (I2 185)

You may possess riches without being poisoned by them, so long as they are in your house or purse only, and not in your heart. (I2 186)

You may take care to increase your wealth and resources, provided this is done not only justly but properly and charitably. (I1 163)

As love of God is sweet, peaceable, and calm, so also the care that proceeds from such love, even if it is for worldly good, is amiable, sweet, and agreeable. (I1 164)

It is not possible to take great pleasure in anything without becoming attached to it. If you lose property, and find yourself grievously afflicted at the loss, you may be sure that you were warmly attached to it;—there is no surer proof of affection for the thing lost than our sorrow at its loss. (I2 188)

If we had nothing else but God, would it not be enough? (L 127)

He wants our misery to be the throne of His mercy, and our powerlessness the seat of His omnipotence. Where did God place the divine strength that He gave to Samson but in his hair, the weakest place in him? (L 142)

Frequently give up some of your property by giving it with a generous heart to the poor.... It is true that God will repay us not only in the next world but even in this. (I1 165)

Nothing makes us so prosperous in this world as to give alms. (I1 165)

Be patient, you are in good company. Our Lord Himself, our Lady, the apostles, and countless saints, both men and women, have been poor. (I1 168)

Spirit of Poverty

Everybody finds themselves sometimes deficient in what they need, and put to inconvenience.... the richest people may easily be without something they want, and that is practically to suffer poverty. Accept such occurrences cheerfully, rejoice in them, bear them willingly. (I2 192)

A man loses nothing by living generously, nobly, courteously, and with a royal, just, and reasonable heart. (I1 217)

You are capable of realising a longing after God, why should you trifle with anything lower? You can live for eternity, why should you stop short in time? (I2 364)

We will soon be in eternity, and then we will see how all the affairs of this world are such little things and how little it matters whether they turn out or not.... We will see that our concerns in this world were truly only child's play. (L 48)

A well-ordered heart will more often ask itself, "What will the angels say if I think of such a thing?" than "What will men say?" (I1 278)

[We should examine how we have acted] in fear of the perils of sin, and of the loss of this world's goods; we fear the one too much and the other too little. (I2 360)

Peace is better than a fortune. You must do what you see can be done with love. (L 54)

The whole world is not worth one soul. (I2 370)

Nothing really counts except the soul. If I could live as long again as I have already lived with the certainty of all the happiness and prosperity which this life can offer, what would it all amount to in the light of eternity? (SFS 86–87)

[In] perfect love of God, . . . we love him above all things. (T 154)

[Our] heart's thirst cannot be slaked in this life and . . . this world is not enough to quench it. (T 189)

Prefer God before all things. (T 204)

In this mortal life all of us are pilgrims. (T 213)

Our Savior's heart is the true oriental pearl, uniquely unique and of priceless value. (T 300)

Do not allow this heavenly spirit to become captive to earthly goods. Let it always remain superior to them and over them, not in them. (I1 162)

Our possessions are not ours,—God has given them to us to cultivate, that we may make them fruitful and profitable in His Service, and so doing we shall please Him. (I2 189)

One single day of devotion is worth more than a thousand years of worldly life. (I2 295)

[God's goodness] only gives.... Our poverty would remain wanting and wretched if the abundance of his goodness did not come to its aid. (T 92)

Of what use will my valor be if I use it only to acquire the transitory things of this mortal life? Certainly, even if I were the strongest and most prudent man in the world, and did not use this valor and prudence for eternal life, it would amount to nothing. (S3 39–40)

Do you think you will remain forever here on earth, or that you are here only to amass temporal goods? Oh clearly, you were not created for that. (S3 72)

It is true that God created the world for man, with the intention that he use the goods he finds in it, but not to enjoy them as if they were his final end.... He created him for a higher end, Himself. (S3 72)

Few are easily parted with what they possess. (S3 73)

There is a great difference between drinking wine and becoming intoxicated, between using riches and adoring them. (S3 74)

We ought to enjoy spiritual things, and only use those which are material. (I2 281)

In order to pray well we must acknowledge that we are poor, and we must greatly humble ourselves.... When we wish our prayer to reach Heaven we must lower ourselves by the awareness of our nothingness. (S1 9–10)

The world is passing away. (S2 104)

More than all earthly pleasures, the loves of Our Lord have an incomparable strength and indescribable power to refresh the human heart.... Nothing is capable of giving it perfect satisfaction except the love of God alone. (S2 137)

Consider, if you will, all the great ones of the earth and consider their condition one after another; you will see that they are never really satisfied. If they are rich and raised to the highest dignities of this world they always desire more. (S2 137)

The Fourth Joyful Mystery

The Presentation in the Temple

Obedience

If you love me, you will keep my commandments.
—John 14:15

You cannot serve God at your will. (L 61)

It is indeed reasonable that we should do His will, for we are in this world only for that.... How can we say we are His, if we are unwilling to accommodate our will to His? (L 7–8)

Serve God as He wishes. You will see that one day He will do all you wish, and more than you know how to wish. (L 165)

Serve and love God well.... This should be our only intention. (II 127)

[God's] choice is always better than our own. (II 141)

If you gather and handle the goods of this world with one hand, you must always hold fast with the other to your heavenly Father's hand and turn toward Him from time to time to see if your actions or occupations are pleasing to Him. (I1 153)

It is a mistake for those who find it hard to pay a willing obedience to their natural superiors to suppose that if they were professed religious they would find it easy to obey. (I2 178)

Blessed indeed are the obedient, for God will never permit them to go astray. (I2 179)

To serve Him as He wishes we must have great care to serve Him well both in great, lofty matters and in small, unimportant things. With love we can capture His heart by the one just as well as by the other. (I1 213)

Serve in spirit the whole court of heaven while joyously carrying out these humble tasks.... Know that such [is] God's will. (I1 214)

❧

The difference between love and devotion is just that which exists between fire and flame ... and what devotion adds to the fire of love is that flame which makes it eager, energetic and diligent, not merely in obeying God's

Commandments, but in fulfilling His Divine Counsels and inspirations. (I2 4–5)

Great occasions for serving God come seldom, but little ones surround us daily. (I2 263)

In proportion as we have less of our own will, that of God is more easily observed. (L 9)

I can in no way approve the idea that a person obligated to a certain duty or vocation should distract himself by longing for any other kind of life but one in keeping with his duties or by engaging in exercises incompatible with his present state. To do so dissipates his heart and renders it unfit for its needed work. (I1 218)

A person who has not the fever of self-will is satisfied with everything, provided that God is served. He cares not in what capacity God employs him, provided that he does the divine will. It is all one to him. (L 9–10)

God has infinite love for obedience. (I1 264)

It is no great merit to serve one's king in the piping days of peace and amid the delights of court life. To serve him during the hardships of war and amid troubles and persecutions is a true mark of constancy and fidelity. (I1 266)

We must leave the choice to God, for it belongs to Him. (SFS 143)

If it is done lovingly, there is no danger in complaining, nor in begging cure, nor in changing place, nor in getting ourselves relieved. But do this with love, and with resignation into the arms of the good will of God. (L 90)

The resolution to prefer God's will before all things is the essential point of sacred love, and that in which the image of eternal love, that is, of the Holy Spirit, is represented. (T 211)

Charity, daughter of heavenly mercy and delight, cannot bear to see her child die, which is the resolution never to offend God. (T 211)

When our will encounters God, it finds rest. (T 241)

Serve God and do what he ordains. The first joins us to God's goodness; the second enables us to fulfill his will. (T 267)

[Until] our senses, interior powers and spiritual faculties... have a ruler, that is, until they have chosen [our Lord] for their king, they are restless. (S4 60)

He whose only concern is to do the divine will obtains from His goodness all that he needs. (S4 77)

Children who have a good father ought to imitate him and follow his commandment in all things. Now, we have a Father better than all others and from whom all good is derived. (S3 96)

Simply go and do what the Lord commands. (S3 173)

Listen to Him carefully. His doctrine is all divine: and if you practice and follow it, it will lead you to eternal life. (S3 185)

Why do some ask for a redemption other than that of the Cross? Is the Cross not sufficient?... This Redemption is so plenteous that it could never be exhausted, not only after millions of years, but even after millions of millions of centuries. (S3 202)

We must reject all that is contrary to obedience, never permitting such movements and inspirations. Simply obey. God does not ask anything else of you. (S3 204)

You who profess the spiritual life know the difference between effective love and affective love.... He does not consider those blest who simply hear His word but only those who also keep it. (S2 26)

Just as a bird would speedily fall to the ground if it did not maintain its flight by repeated strokes of its wings..., you need frequently to reiterate the good resolutions you have made to serve God. (I2 346)

The Fifth Joyful Mystery

The Finding of the Child Jesus in the Temple

❧

Piety

You ... must be perfect as your heavenly Father is perfect.
—Matthew 5:48

As the mother-of-pearl lives in the sea without ever absorbing one drop of salt water ... even so a true stedfast soul may live in the world untainted by worldly breath, finding a well-spring of holy piety amid the bitter waves of society, and hovering amid the flames of earthly lusts without singeing the wings of its devout life. (I2 vi–vii)

Grace ... makes us acceptable to His Divine Majesty;—when it strengthens us to do well, it is called Charity;—but when it attains its fullest perfection, in which it not only leads us to do well, but to act carefully, diligently, and promptly, then it is called Devotion. (I2 3)

Have wings to soar aloft to God in holy prayer and ... feet to walk among men in a holy and lovable way of life. (I1 43)

Piety

When God created the world He commanded each tree to bear fruit after its kind; and even so He bids Christians,—the living trees of His Church,—to bring forth fruits of devotion, each one according to his kind and vocation. (I2 8)

Devotion which is true hinders nothing, but on the contrary it perfects everything; and that which runs counter to the rightful vocation of any one is, you may be sure, a spurious devotion. (I2 9)

[Have] special and particular resolutions for your own correction and improvement.... In this way you will correct your faults in a short time. (I1 88–89)

Be sure that wheresoever our lot is cast we may and must aim at the perfect life. (I2 11)

Hasten to put inspiration into practice. This is the height of true virtue. To have consent within your heart without putting it into effect is like planting a vine with no intention that it bear fruit. (I1 111)

In practicing the virtues we should prefer the one most conformable to our duties rather than the one more agreeable to our tastes. (I1 122)

Pious souls who undertake some special devout practice use it as the ground of their spiritual embroidery, and frame all manner of other graces upon it, ordering their actions and affections better by means of this their chief thread which runs through all. (I2 129)

※

By perfect practice of a single virtue a person can reach the heights in all virtue. (I1 124)

Our business only is to become good, devout people, pious men and women; and all our efforts must be to that end. (I2 134)

Affairs of importance do not give us as much trouble as do many trifling things. Undertake all your affairs with a calm mind and try to dispatch them in order one after the other. (I1 152)

All of us are obliged to practice these three virtues [obedience, chastity, and poverty], although not all in the same way. (I1 154)

Whoever has Jesus Christ in his heart will soon have Him in all his outward ways. (I1 184)

To meet frequently with such [devout and virtuous persons] will be of the very greatest benefit to you. (I1 190)

To speak little—a practice highly recommended by ancient sages—does not consist in uttering only a few words but in uttering none that are useless. (I1 207)

Put your hand to strong things, by training yourself in prayer and meditation and receiving the sacraments.
(I1 214–15)

We do not very often come across opportunities for exercising strength, magnanimity, or magnificence; but gentleness, temperance, modesty, and humility are graces which ought to colour everything we do. (I2 125)

To live according to God is to love. (T 122)

If we accepted his inspirations to the full extent of their power in how short a time would we make great progress in holiness! (T 129)

True virtue has no limits; it goes ever forward. Above all others, holy charity... would be capable of becoming infinite if it found a heart capable of infinity. (T 164)

Little deeds that proceed from charity please God and have their place among meritorious acts. (T 166)

A just soul is the spouse of our Lord. (T 169)

As long as charity is in us it produces many acts of love of God. By the frequent exercise of such acts our soul acquires a certain habit and custom of loving God.
(T 225–26)

To speak well, it is enough to love well. (S4 xviii)

It is our works and not our words that give testimony to what we are. (S4 10)

It is not enough to be called a Christian if we do not perform the works of a Christian. (S4 11)

God has not placed perfection in the multiplicity of acts we perform to please Him, but only in the way we perform them, which is simply to do the little we do according to our vocation, in love, by love, and for love. (S3 29)

Transformation is the true mark of a divine visitation. (S2 170)

All are called to perfection, since Our Lord was speaking to all when He said: "Be perfect as your Heavenly Father is perfect." (S3 120)

If when we consecrate ourselves to God's service we begin by absolutely and unreservedly entrusting our spirit into His hands, how happy we will be! Any delay in our perfection comes from this lack of self-gift. (S3 205)

Our business is to love what God would have done. He wills our vocation as it is. Let us love that and not trifle away our time hankering after other people's vocations. (V 6)

When is the most fitting time for us to consecrate and devote ourselves to God? It is the present moment, now, immediately; for the past is no longer ours, the future may never be ours, so the present moment is the best. (S2 42)

We must get used to seeking the attainment of our perfection by the ordinary ways, in tranquility of heart, ... each of us according to our condition and vocation. (S2 97)

To remain stationary for a long time is impossible. The man who makes no gain loses in such traffic as this. The man who does not climb upward goes down on this ladder. (T 163)

To be perfect in our vocation is nothing else than to fulfil the duties which our state of life obliges us to perform, and to accomplish them well, and only for the honor and love of God. (V 2)

Jesus is the teacher of holiness. I go to Him because I want Him to teach me how to become a saint. Of what use to me is all I learn in school if I do not become holy? (V 107)

THE SORROWFUL MYSTERIES

The First Sorrowful Mystery

The Agony of Jesus in the Garden

☙

Sorrow for Sin

The cares of the world, and the delight in riches, and the desire for other things, enter in and choke the word, and it proves unfruitful.—Mark 4:19

A soul that hopes for the honor of being made spouse of the Son of God must "put off the old man, and put on the new" by forsaking sin and removing and cutting away whatever obstructs union with God. (I1 47)

No matter how slight contrition may be, provided only that it is genuine, and especially when it is joined to the power of the sacraments, it cleanses us sufficiently from sin. (I1 51–52)

Consider His spiritual gifts.... how often He has forgiven you, how often delivered you from occasions of falling; what opportunities He has granted for your soul's progress! Dwell somewhat on the detail; see how Loving and Gracious God has been to you. (I2 30–31)

Ask pardon and, like the prodigal son, like Magdalen ...cast yourself at the feet of the Lord...[the] living fountain of compassion. (I1 59)

Turn anew, without any delay, to seek His Divine Mercy. (I2 55)

Venial sins do not kill the soul but spoil its devotion and so entangle its powers in bad habits and inclinations that it can no longer exert the prompt charity that constitutes devotion. (I1 76)

The examination of conscience must always be made before going to bed.... If we have done anything wrong in thought, word, or deed, we must ask pardon of His Divine Majesty with a firm resolution to confess it at the first opportunity and to make careful amendment for it. (I1 95–96)

As we reflect on our sins one by one let us also consider His graces one by one. (I1 135)

Sorrow may be good or bad according to the several results it produces in us. And indeed there are more bad than good results arising from it, for the only good ones are mercy and repentance. (I2 319)

We must be sorry for our faults, but in a calm, settled, firm way.... We correct ourselves much better by calm, steady repentance than by that which is harsh, turbulent, and passionate. (I1 150)

❦

Let us start out again on the way of humility. Let us be of good heart and from this day be more on guard. God will help us; we will do better. (I1 151)

When you have fallen, lift up your heart in quietness, humbling yourself deeply before God by reason of your frailty, without marvelling that you fell;—there is no cause to marvel because weakness is weak, or infirmity infirm. (I2 172)

Detest your sins for they alone can ruin you. (I1 63)

At first you may suffer somewhat under the loss of what you enjoyed among your vain, frivolous companions; but would you forfeit the eternal gifts of God for such things as these? (I2 294–95)

If, after an honest investigation of our own conduct, we find the cause of our wrongdoing, we must thank God, for an evil is half cured when we have found out its cause. (I2 335–36)

The Enemy makes use of sadness to try good men with his temptations:—just as he tries to make bad men merry in their sin, so he seeks to make the good sorrowful amid their works of piety. (I2 320)

If you allow appetite to carry you into sin, then you will be under it and it will have mastery over you. (T 57)

One can scarcely be ignorant [of the riches of God's goodness]. Indeed this rich, full, and plenteous sufficiency of means which God freely bestows on sinners so that they can love him is seen almost everywhere in Scripture. (T 123)

Self-love hinders reason. (I2 264)

He will not raise us up without our co-operation. (T 134)

Sin is an offense against God, just as virtue is honor paid to him. (T 149)

Do you not see that all such acts of repentance are made for the sake of our own soul, its happiness, its inner beauty, its honor, its dignity, in a word for self-love? (T 152)

Be repentant out of love of God.... What father would not take it ill if his son was willing enough to serve him but never with love or out of love? (T 152)

[The] first movement which God makes "in us but without us" [is] when he stirs us up and awakens us from the sleep of sin. How could we ask to be awakened, since no man can pray before he is awakened? (T 158)

God by progressive stages filled with unutterable sweetness leads the soul forward and enables it to leave the Egypt of sin. He leads it from love to love, as from dwelling to dwelling, until he has made it enter into the promised land. (T 160)

With unrivaled mercy he opens the heart's door by means of those remorseful stings of conscience which come from the various kinds of light and knowledge he casts into our souls. (T 169–70)

Still venial sin is sin, and consequently it disturbs charity. (T 205)

A man who does not have much love for his country is not greatly troubled if it is ruined. A man who has scarcely any love for God has scarcely any more hatred for sin. (T 303)

Although no one can be exempt from temptation, still no one should seek it or go of his own accord to the place where it may be found. (S3 15)

When sinners are most hardened in their sins, when they have reached the point of living as if there were no God, no Heaven or Hell, it is often then that the Lord allows them to find His Heart full of pity and kind mercy toward them. (S4 43)

Circumcise your heart by cutting off evil language, friendships and conversations; cut off this evil flirting and other such foolishness. Begin there if you want to undergo a good circumcision. (S4 89–90)

Do not hope to be able to live without committing imperfections, seeing that this is impossible while you are in this life. It is enough that you do not love them and that they do not remain in your heart. (S3 25)

[Do] not be astonished or troubled at seeing that we are subject to fall into these imperfections, even often. We must rather confide ourselves to the goodness of God who, for all that, does not love us less. (S3 27)

The good thief... at the end of his life looked at the Cross, found redemption there and was saved. His salvation was immediate, for Our Lord had promised that whoever looked upon His Cross, no matter how sinful he might be, even if he did so only at the end of his life, as did the good thief, would receive salvation. (S3 194–95)

Why should a sinner... fear in life and in death to return to his God?... Those who look upon the Cross, no matter how sinful they are, will find salvation and redemption. (S3 195–96)

Our self love... will die only when we die, it will live as long as we live; but it is enough if it does not reign in us. (S2 45)

The motive of perfect repentance... is God's goodness and we are displeased at having offended it. (T 155)

Who will dare to measure, by the greatness of his sins, the immensity of that infinite mercy which casts them all into the depths of the sea of oblivion, when we repent of them with love? (V 76)

In the matter of evil, he who has a little is not contented, and he who has much is discontented; but he who has a little virtue is gladsome, and his gladness is for ever greater as he goes on. (I2 365)

The Second Sorrowful Mystery

The Scourging at the Pillar

Purity

Clean the inside of cup and dish first so that the outside may become clean as well.—Matthew 23:26

For us the beginning of good health is to be purged of our sinful tendencies. (I₁ 47)

The work of purging the soul neither can nor should end except with our life itself. We must not be disturbed at our imperfections, since for us perfection consists in fighting against them. (I₁ 48)

How can we fight against [our imperfections] unless we see them, or overcome them unless we face them? Our victory does not consist in being unconscious of them but in not consenting to them. (I₁ 48)

The same light that enables us to see such defects and blemishes inflames us with desire to cleanse and purify ourselves of them. (I₁ 75)

We can never be altogether free from venial sin,—at least not until after a very long persistence in this purity; but we can be without any affection for venial sin. (I2 58)

It is a pity to sow the seed of vain and foolish tastes in the soil of your heart, taking up the place of better things, and hindering the soul from cultivating good dispositions. (I2 61)

There are few people in whom we may not observe some such imperfections.... Though they are peculiar and natural to each of us, by care and a contrary affection we can correct and restrain them and even completely purify and free ourselves of them. (I1 78–79)

Nothing so much as prayer so effectively purifies our intellect of ignorance and our will of depraved affections. (I1 81)

Purity is the lily among virtues—by it men approach to the Angels. There is no beauty without purity, and human purity is chastity. (I2 180)

[Chastity] has its own peculiar glory of being the fair, unspotted virtue of both soul and body. (I1 156)

❧

A chaste heart is like the mother-of-pearl, which cannot admit any drop of water except that which comes down from heaven, for it can take no pleasure except that of marriage which is ordained by heaven. (I1 156)

In order to receive God's Grace in our hearts, they must be as empty vessels—not filled with self-esteem. (I2 142-43)

Resist impure images.... Pure souls must be on guard and never doubt that chastity is incomparably finer than anything incompatible with it. (I1 157)

Our Blessed Lord Himself has promised the special blessing of beholding Him to those that are pure in heart. (I2 182)

Be very quick to turn away from whatever leads or allures to lewd conduct, for this evil works without our knowing it and from small beginnings moves on to great difficulties. Such things are always easier to avoid than to cure. (I1 159)

Do you, in your folly, imagine that you can lightly handle love as you please? You think to trifle with it, but it will sting you cruelly. (I2 200)

Do not associate with immodest persons, especially if they are also loose in speech, as is generally the case. (I1 161)

Satan... tries to introduce impurity by almost insensible degrees. (I1 177)

Purity

Always keep yourself close to Jesus Christ crucified, both spiritually by meditation and really by Holy Communion.... If you rest your heart on our Lord, who is the true chaste and immaculate Lamb, you will see that your soul and your heart will soon be cleansed of all stain and lewdness. (I1 161)

Make yourself every day more pure of heart. This purity consists in estimating and weighing all things in the balance of that sanctuary, which is nothing other than the will of God. (L 19–20)

Chaste friendship is at all times and in all ways honest, courteous, and amiable. It never changes except into a purer and more perfect union of minds, a living image of the blessed friendship that exists in heaven. (I1 178)

All the temptations of hell cannot stain a soul that does not love them. (L 214–215)

It is a good sign when the devil makes so much noise and tempest round about the will. It is a sign that he is not within. (L 209)

When young people indulge in looks, words or actions which they would not like to be seen by their parents, husbands or confessors, it is a sure sign that they are damaging their conscience and their honour. (I2 207–8)

The heart and ear are closely allied, and just as you would vainly seek to check the downward course of a mountain torrent, so difficult will you find it to keep the smooth words which enter in at the ear from finding their way down into the heart. (I2 209)

God bids you deal chiefly with your heart, for that is the chief offender. (I2 222)

Not only in body but in heart as well, no ornament becomes [you like] humility, modesty and devotion. (I1 192)

Our words are a true test of the state of our soul. (I2 230)

Examine what attachments hinder your spiritual life, what passions engross it, and what chiefly attracts you. It is by testing the passions of the soul, one by one, that we ascertain our spiritual condition. (I2 360)

By simple chastity we lend our body to God. (I1 230)

Our Lord does not say "blessed are the clean of body," but rather the clean "of heart"; and He praises not "the poor," but "the poor in spirit." (L 135)

How is your heart with regard to venial sin? We cannot keep ourselves so pure as not to fall now and then into such sins, but is there any of them to which you have a particular inclination? (I₁ 276)

How is your heart with regard to spiritual exercises? Do you like them? Do you esteem them or do they make you ill at ease?... If you note anything to which your heart has less inclination, look for the source of such dislike and discover its cause. (I₁ 276)

Like Naaman, we come out of the stream of salvation more pure and clean than if we had never had leprosy. This is to the end that God's majesty...should not "be overcome by evil, but overcome evil by good." (T 116)

There are few vines that do not need to be pruned of leaves and buds. (T 40)

A Christian must love his body as a living image of his incarnate Savior, as having issued with him from the same stock, and consequently belonging to him in parentage and blood. (T 183)

Eyes, ears, and mouth are the doors of the soul. (T 310)

Just as He permits sin, He sends infirmities to correct and purify us of it. Thus, we must be submissive to His justice as well as to His mercy.... This will make us tranquilly embrace the events of His providence. (S₃ 110)

We must be very careful in the practice of modesty.
(S2 71)

It often happens that once an evil object has effectively cast its allurements into our heart, we become attached to it with excessive complacence. When this complacence increases we can hardly rid ourselves of it. (T 207)

The Third Sorrowful Mystery

The Crowning with Thorns

🌑

Courage

Courage! It is I! Do not be afraid.
—Matthew 14:27

In this enterprise we must have courage and patience. (I1 48)

Fortunately for us, in this war we are always victorious provided that we are willing to fight. (I1 49)

Always have at hand some approved book of devotion. ...Read a little of them every day with great devotion, just as if you were reading a letter that the saints had sent you from heaven to show you the way and give you the courage to go there. (I1 108)

The proud man who trusts in himself may well undertake nothing, but the humble man is all the braver that he knows his own helplessness...because all his trust is in God, Who delights to show forth His Power in our weakness, His Mercy in our misery. (I2 151)

By means of the continued practice of prayer, the sacraments, and confidence in God, our strength will return and we will live a healthful and happy life. (I1 244)

Fear is a greater evil than the evil itself.... Fear not; you walk on the sea, amid the winds and the waves, but it is with Jesus. (L 149)

Our enemy is a great clatterer; do not trouble yourself at all about him.... He has howled round about the saints, and made plenty of hubbub, but to what purpose? In spite of it all, there they are, seated in the place that he has lost, the wretch! (L 137)

Let us say to God, "Father, if it is possible, let this chalice pass from me," but let us courageously add, "But not my will, but Yours be done." (I1 265)

We must patiently suffer the aridity itself, since God has ordained it for the development of our interior virtue. We must never lose courage during these interior troubles. (I1 268)

[Strive] most ardently for the glory of God and of the Church. The stage [is] small, but the action great. (T 46)

꽃

Just as possession of the good gives joy to the heart, so also victory over evil gratifies a courageous spirit. (T 59)

This horde of passions is let stay in our souls…in order to develop our will in spiritual strength and valor. (T 59)

Go forward…and set up no other limits than those of your life. As long as life lasts run after your Savior. But run ardently and swiftly, for what will it avail you to follow him if you are not so happy as to reach him? (T 164)

Strong and healthy men must often be stirred up to put their strength and skill to proper use. (T 171)

We ought to have great courage and most firm confidence in God and in his assistance. If we do not fail to respond to his grace, he will accomplish in us the good work of our salvation. (T 174)

[God] wills that by resistance our charity may be practiced more fully, that by combat we may gain victory, and that by victory we may obtain triumph. (T 207–8)

Many who have had great distrust of their strength and great fear of failing on trial, when the time came have suddenly done wonders, because this great sense of their weakness has urged them to seek the aid and succor of God. (L 218–19)

Just as many men have lost courage during an actual attack, so also in the presence of danger and difficulty many men have lost their fears and have gained courage and resolution which otherwise they could never have had. (T 231)

It is sufficient to desire courage and trust that God will give it to us at the necessary time. Samson did not always have courage. (T 231)

It is not necessary for us always to have the feeling and movement of courage.... It is enough that we have a right desire to fight valiantly together with perfect confidence that the Spirit of God will assist us with his help when occasion to use it presents itself. (T 231)

As long as we live we will have passions.... It is precisely in the struggle with these passions and emotions that our victory and triumph lies. (S4 94)

Let us leave the blind world to make as much noise as it may...; let us be firm in our ways, unchangeable in our resolutions, and perseverance will be the test of our self-surrender to God. (I2 293)

It is the very essence of the perfection of that Heavenly Love to require its lovers to endure and fight for Love's sake. (I2 302)

If we feel that we lack courage let us cry out in a loud voice full of confidence, "Lord, save me!" Let us not doubt that God will strengthen us and prevent us from perishing. (S3 22)

Remain in peace and do not trouble yourself about the perfection you so much desire. It will be enough if you have it in dying. Be not timid! Walk confidently! If you are armed with the armor of faith, nothing can harm you. (S3 25)

Courage then! Let us rouse our faith again, and give it life through charity, and the practices and good works performed in charity. (S3 50)

Have patience, lay aside a bit of that anxious care of yourselves, and have no fear that anything will be wanting to you. For if you trust in God, He will take care of you and everything necessary for your perfection. (S3 119)

Christians ought to walk under the standard of God's Providence and be ready to embrace all the effects and events of this kind Providence.... Let us not be carried away by disturbing and morose fears. (S3 141)

Let us rather have a fear which keeps us prepared and always ready to die well.... The general rule for a good death is to lead a good life. (S3 142)

Persevere in good.... Let the world cry out as much as it wants; let human prudence censure and condemn our actions as much as it desires;... let us not be frightened or give up; let us rather pursue our course firmly and faithfully. (S3 166)

Considering what our Head and Captain has done, are we going to be cowardly soldiers, weak in courage? (S2 109)

Love never says: "Enough, sufficient." It desires to have the courage always to progress on the way of the will of the Beloved. (S2 152)

What is there to fear? But if fear seizes you, cry loudly, "O Lord, save me." He will give you His hand: clasp it tight, and go joyously on. (L 149)

Let us go in the safekeeping of God. (SFS 145)

The Fourth Sorrowful Mystery

The Carrying of the Cross

☙

Patience

[A]s for the [seeds] in the good soil, they are those who, hearing the word, hold it fast in an honest and good heart, and bring forth fruit with patience.—Luke 8:15

The soul that rises from sin to devotion has been compared to the dawning day, which at its approach does not drive out the darkness instantaneously but only little by little. (I1 48)

A slow cure, as the maxim says, is always surest. Diseases of the soul as well as those of the body come posting on horseback but leave slowly and on foot. (I1 48)

He will unfailingly be pleased with our patience and take note of our diligence and perseverance. (I1 93)

Love ought to reign, and little by little love drives out servile fear. (I1 125)

The greatest happiness of any one is "to possess his soul;" and the more perfect our patience, the more fully we do so possess our souls. (I2 136)

Be patient not only with regard to the big, chief part of the afflictions that may come to you but also as to things accompanying them and accidental circumstances. Many people would be ready to accept evils provided they were not inconvenienced by them. (I1 129)

If we must have patience with others, so we must with ourselves. Those who aspire to the pure love of God have not so much need of patience with others as with themselves. (L 170)

God will work with you, in you, and for you, and after your labor consolation will follow. (I1 153)

The truly patient man neither complains of his hard lot nor desires to be pitied by others. He speaks of his sufferings in a natural, true, and sincere way, without murmuring, complaining, or exaggerating them. (I1 130)

Turn your thoughts to some good, commendable activity. When such thoughts enter and find place in your heart, they will drive away temptations and evil thoughts. (I1 246)

Patience

Take patiently the petty annoyances, the trifling discomforts, the unimportant losses which come upon all of us daily; for by means of these little matters, lovingly and freely accepted, you will give Him your whole heart, and win His. (I2 261)

The acts of daily forbearance, the headache, or toothache, or heavy cold; the tiresome peculiarities of husband or wife, the broken glass... all of these sufferings, small as they are, if accepted lovingly, are most pleasing to God's Goodness. (I2 261)

Do not desire faraway things, that is, things that cannot happen for a long time, as many people do, and by so doing wear out and waste their hearts to no purpose and expose themselves to the danger of becoming very discontented. (I1 217)

Perseverance will prove whether we have sincerely sacrificed ourselves to God and dedicated ourselves to a devout life. (I1 237)

Hypocrisy is short-lived, and disperses like a mist, while real goodness is firm and abiding. (I2 293)

If we walk steadily and faithfully..., God will lift us up to greater things. (I2 136)

Although great temptations exceed in quality, small ones immeasurably exceed in number so that victory over them may be comparable to that gained over greater temptations. (I1 247)

Just as internal commotions and seditions ruin a commonwealth, and make it incapable of resisting its foreign enemies, so if our heart be disturbed and anxious, it loses power to retain such graces as it has, as well as strength to resist the Evil One, who is all the more ready to fish (according to an old proverb) in troubled waters. (I2 316–17)

With the single exception of sin, anxiety is the greatest evil that can happen to a soul. (I1 251)

Continue the devout life, as you have begun, and go always from well to better in the road in which you are; and you will see that after some time these errors will grow weak and will not trouble you so much. (L 107–8)

Oppose vigorously any tendency to sadness.... You must persevere. By means of sorrow the enemy tries to make us weary of good works, but if he sees that we don't give them up and that being done in spite of his opposition they have become very meritorious, he will stop troubling us. (I1 254)

During the night we must wait for the light. (I1 268)

We must resolve to stand fast in a holy love of God even though we may never find any consolation through–

out our whole life. We must be ready, as ready on Mt. Calvary as on Mount Tabor, to say, "Lord, it is good for me to be with you, whether you are on the Cross or in your glory." (I1 261)

Practice serving our Lord with a gentleness full of strength and zeal. That is the true method of this service. Wish not to do all, but only something, and without doubt you will do much. (L 153)

Fruits that ripen late keep better than those that ripen early. (SFS 67)

Be satisfied if from time to time you win some small victory over your besetting sin. We must bear with other people, but still more must we bear with ourselves and have patience with our own failures. (SFS 136–37)

How can we expect to achieve inward tranquility without passing through the usual struggles and contradictions? (SFS 137)

Never be hurried in anything. Do all things calmly and in a spirit of repose. Do not lose your inward peace even if everything seems to be going wrong. What is anything in life compared to peace of soul? (SFS 157)

Love...makes [us] keep to the road and finish the journey. (T 68)

God's favor floats as it were over all this and finds joy in turning all these miseries to the greater profit of those who love him. From toil he makes patience spring forth. (T 115)

Patience is more perfect as it is less mixed with disquiet and eagerness. May God then deign to deliver you from these two troubles. (L 205)

What is the prize if it is not Jesus Christ? How can you take hold of him if you do not follow him? (T 164)

He enables [his children] to walk before him; he holds their hand in difficulties; he himself carries them along in hardships that he sees as being otherwise unbearable to them. (T 173–74)

We must unceasingly ask for [perseverance] by making use of the means which God has taught us for obtaining it: prayer, fasting, almsgiving, frequenting the sacraments, association with good companions, and hearing and reading Holy Scripture. (T 175)

Be patient and one day you will be in Heaven, where there will be only peace and joy.... You will possess an enduring tranquility and rest. (S4 93–94)

Our entire good consists not only in accepting the truth of God's word, but in persevering in it. (S3 152)

He who desires to be patient must be humble, because one cannot long support the labors and adversities of this life without the humility which makes us gentle and patient. (S3 172)

Patience will win for [you] perpetual peace and tranquility.... [You] shall be covered with the hundredfold of blessings in this life and shall bless the Father, Son and Holy Spirit eternally in the next. (S3 175)

The virtue of patience is the one which most assures us of perfection. (V 120)

He would never exhort the faithful to persevere if he were not ready to give them the power to do so. (T 176)

The Fifth Sorrowful Mystery

The Crucifixion

Self-Denial

If any man would come after me, let him deny himself and take up his cross daily and follow me.—Luke 9:23

When you are sick, offer all your pains and weakness to our Dear Lord, and ask Him to unite them to the sufferings which He bore for you. (I2 141)

How holy, my dear daughter, and how agreeable to God we should be, if we knew how to use properly the subjects of mortification that our vocation affords! (L 89)

Where there is the least of our will, there is the most of God's. Simple, pure acceptance of God's will makes our suffering pure in the highest degree. (I1 168)

If you can stand fasting, you will do well to fast on certain days in addition to those prescribed by the Church. (I1 185)

Self-Denial

The usual effects of fasting [are], namely, elevating our spirits, keeping the body in subjection, practicing virtue, and gaining a greater reward in heaven. (I1 185)

Although we may be able to do but little, the enemy nevertheless stands more in awe of those whom he knows can fast. (I2 217)

Our good God sometimes tries our courage and our love, depriving us of the things that seem to us, and which really are, very good for the soul. And if He sees us ardent in their pursuit, and yet humble, tranquil, and resigned to doing without…He gives us blessings greater in the privation than in the possession of the thing desired. (L 3–4)

Trials [are]…a great source of merit and profit for you and have greatly increased your strength and virtue. (I1 242)

Both fasting and labor mortify and subdue the flesh. If your work is necessary for you to contribute to God's glory, I much prefer that you endure the pains of work rather than of fasting. (I1 185–86)

Practice the mortifications that most often present themselves to you; for this is the thing we must do first. (L 153)

It is no little mortification to adapt our taste to all kinds of food and keep it under control at all times. Mortification of this kind doesn't show in public, bothers no one, and is well adapted to social life. (I1 186)

Do not desire crosses, unless you have borne those already laid upon you well—it is an abuse to long after martyrdom while unable to bear an insult patiently. (I2 269)

Our actions are like roses, which, though they may be more beautiful when fresh, have a sweeter and stronger scent when they are dried..., but when they are done amid dryness and deadness they are more precious in God's Sight. (I2 339)

It is a true sign of love to deprive ourselves of something for the sake of the one we love. What have you given up out of love of God? (I1 278)

Consider the love with which Jesus Christ our Lord has suffered so much in this world, especially in the Garden of Olives and on Mount Calvary. That love was for you. (I1 285)

The Heart of our most Dear Lord beheld you from the tree of the Cross and loved you, and by that Love He won for you all good things which you were ever to have, and amongst them your good resolutions. (I2 367–68)

He willed...to make himself companion of our miseries so as afterwards to make us companions of his glory. (T 113)

Always add new good works to those already done, for the coins out of which your treasures must be made are fasting, prayer, and almsgiving. (T 166)

He gives us both his death and his life: his life so that we may be freed from eternal death, his death so that we can enjoy eternal life. (T 178–79)

Experience as many ecstasies, spiritual raptures and transports as you wish; even ravish the Eternal Father's Heart if you are able. Yet if with all this you do not dwell on the Savior's Cross and practice self-mortification, I assure you that all the rest is absolutely nothing and will disappear in smoke and vanity. (S4 15)

In proportion as you are hindered from doing the good you desire, do the good that you do not desire...they are worth more. (L 62)

Make straight the way of the Lord, that is, acquire an even disposition by the mortification of your passions, inclinations and aversions. An even disposition is the most pleasing virtue in the spiritual life, one for which we must work continuously. (S4 47–48)

He could have saved the world without shedding His blood, but that would not have been enough to satisfy the love He bears us. (S4 99)

It is not enough to fast exteriorly if we do not also fast interiorly and if we do not accompany the fast of the body with that of the spirit. (S3 2)

If we have offended God through the eyes, through the ears, through the tongue, and through our other senses, why should we not make them fast as well? (S3 3)

We ought to hold in check all those things which keep us from loving or tending to the Sovereign Good. In this way interior fasting accompanies exterior fasting. (S3 3)

Our Lord willed to be tempted during the forty days He was in the desert precisely in order to teach us that we shall also be tempted during the entire time that we dwell in the desert of this mortal life. (S3 25)

[Be] trained in the school of the crucifix. (T 131)

We shall never be capable of keeping company with Him in His consolations, nor be invited to His heavenly banquet, if we are not sharers of His labors and sufferings. (S3 31)

With an insatiable ardor He desired that everyone be converted at the price of His Passion. Seeing how many souls would not, He cried out: I thirst! (S3 201)

Self-Denial

Love desired that death should enter into Our Lord, so that by His death, love could be spread abroad into all people.... He died of love, this Savior of my soul. (S2 10)

Why should we desire to be masters of ourselves in what concerns the spirit when we are not so in what concerns the body? (S2 30)

God is not satisfied with our offerings when they are not accompanied by that of our own heart... The Divine Majesty asks first for our heart. (S2 45)

This is the aim in religion, for in this consists Christian perfection: to die to self so perfectly that we can say with the Apostle: "The life I live now is not my own; Christ is living in me." (S2 111)

As long as you live you will always find something of yourself to renounce.... We must not grow weary in this work, for we ought to begin and end the spiritual life with the renunciation of our self-will. (S2 111)

All our happiness consists in this subjection of our own spirit, as on the contrary all our unhappiness comes from a lack of it. (S2 112)

It sometimes seems to us that we have been abandoned by God.... To think that we can be devout without suffering is a delusion. Where there is more difficulty, there is more virtue. (S2 171)

THE
GLORIOUS
MYSTERIES

The First Glorious Mystery

The Resurrection of Jesus from the Dead

❦

Faith

Blessed are those who have not seen and yet believe.
—John 20:29

The same Everlasting Father who cares for you today will take care of you tomorrow and every day of your life. Either He will shield you from suffering, or He will give you unfailing strength to bear it. Be at peace then, and put aside all anxious thoughts. (V 132)

He is "the light of the world," and therefore it is in Him and by Him and for Him that we must be instructed and enlightened. He is the tree of desire in whose shade we must be refreshed. (II 81)

God is in all things and all places. There is no place or thing in this world where He is not truly present. Just as wherever birds fly they always encounter the air, so also wherever we go or wherever we are we find God present. (II 84)

Do not philosophize about your trouble, do not turn in upon yourself; go straight on. No, God cannot lose you, so long as you live in your resolution not to lose Him. (L 149)

If He is with me I care not where I go. (L 228)

By surrendering our reputation together with our soul into God's hands, we safeguard it in the best way possible. (I1 145)

Worry disturbs reason and good judgment and prevents us from doing well the very things we are worried about. (I1 152)

When we find that we have been aroused to anger we must call for God's help like the apostles when they were tossed about by the wind and storm on the waters. He will command your passions to cease and there will be a great calm. (I1 148)

You can have no doubt about whether God regards you with love, for He regards lovingly the most horrible sinners in the world on the smallest true desire they have of conversion. (L 182)

Perfect love implies absolute trust in the person loved. (I2 275)

Stretch out your hand to Him like a little child to His father so that He may lead you on. (I1 98)

Do not think that you will be able to succeed in your affairs by your own efforts, but only by the assistance of God; and on setting out, consign yourself to His care, believing that He will do that which will be best for you. (L 47–48)

God takes pleasure to see you take your little steps; and like a good father who holds his child by the hand, He will accommodate His steps to yours and will be content to go no faster than you. Why do you worry? (L 31)

We always do enough when God works with us. (I1 290)

When did His love for you begin? It began even when He began to be God. When did He begin to be God? Never, for He has been forever.... He has always loved you from all eternity and for this reason He has prepared for you all these graces and favors. (I1 286)

Determine to be faithful in making good use of [holy resolutions]. Such means are frequency in prayer, the sacraments, and good works. (I1 287)

Where there is more blessedness, there is more satisfaction. Hence God's goodness takes more pleasure in giving his graces than we have in receiving them. (T 92)

Love and faithfulness lead to familiarity and confidence. (I2 276)

The divine goodness has not called you to the state in which you find yourself without strengthening you for all this. (L 207)

What the world would call a chance or fortuitous event was called by Joseph a design of God's providence, which turns and reduces all things to its service. This holds for all things that take place in the world. (T 110)

He thinks of you, and not only of you, but of the "least hair of your head." This is an article of faith, and we may not have the least doubt of it. (L 181)

God does not extend merely sufficient remedies to convert the obstinate; to this end he dispenses the riches of his goodness. (T 123)

Faith makes us know with infallible certitude that God exists, that he is infinite in goodness, that he can communicate himself to us, and that not only can he do so but he will do so. (T 141)

To believe is to be drawn. Hence he admonishes those who have been aroused to believe in God to ask for the gift of faith. (T 158)

Let us be his both by faith and by works, and he will be ours by glory. (T 178)

It is impossible to look upon the divinity and not to love it. However, here below we do not see it, but only have a glimpse of it through the shadows of faith, seeing it as "in a mirror." (T 203)

Just as God is the maker and father of all things, so also he takes care of all things by his providence which sustains and embraces the whole created machine. (T 223–24)

It is sufficient for us to be faithful during present events according to changing times. Each season has quite enough toil and trouble of its own. (T 230)

[God] is infinitely better than [you] can either desire or even conceive. (T 254)

Our Lord came Himself to teach us what we ought to do. How happy we will be if we imitate Him faithfully and follow His example. (S4 57)

Do you want to know if your faith is dead or dying? Examine your works and actions. (S3 36)

A single one of His sighs would have been enough to redeem not only this world but a thousand worlds, and a thousand thousand human and angelic natures.... Our

Lord merited more by the breath of a single loving sigh than all the saints, all the cherubim and all the seraphim could ever merit. (S4 78)

It [the name of Jesus] is a name which is above every other name, wholly divine, gentle and full of goodness. It is an oil poured out to heal all the wounds of our souls. (S4 102)

It [the name of Jesus] is the name which gives joy to the angels, saves men, and causes demons to tremble. This is why it should be deeply engraved upon our hearts and our spirits. (S4 102)

Faith has for its object the truths revealed by God or the Church, and it is nothing else but an adhesion of our understanding to these truths which it finds both beautiful and good. (S3 34)

Vigilant faith . . . not only observes what is necessary for salvation, but it seeks out, embraces and practices faithfully everything that can bring it closer to its God. (S3 41)

Grace is never wanting. God always gives sufficient grace to whoever is willing to receive it. (S3 67)

When we abandon all to Him, He takes a tender care of us, and His Providence for us is great or small according to the measure of our abandonment. (S3 118)

We must be very faithful, but without anxiety or eagerness; we must use the means that are given to us according to our vocation, and then remain in peace concerning all the rest. For God... will always be attentive to provide us with whatever is necessary. (S3 120)

He asks for your own heart. Give it such as it is.... Are we not aware that everything that is remitted into His divine hands is converted to good? (S2 79)

Who now will have any doubt as to our abundant means of salvation since we have so great a Savior, in view of whom we have been made and by whose merits we have been ransomed? (T 115)

The Second Glorious Mystery

The Ascension of Jesus into Heaven

❦

Hope

Ask, and it will be given you; seek, and you will find; knock, and it will be opened to you.—Luke 11:9

From the heights of heaven Jesus Christ mercifully looks down upon you and graciously invites you there. (I1 67)

Love is the great healer of all ills. (I2 238)

Blessed will be the soul that can truly say to our Lord: "You are my place of strength and my stronghold to give me safety, my roof against the rain, my shade against the heat." (I1 97)

If you have firm trust in God, the success that comes to you will always be that which is most useful for you whether it appears good or bad in your private judgment. (I1 153)

When you give yourself to Him you win both Him and yourself for eternal life. (I1 74)

To trust in God when one is destitute of such support is worthy of great praise. (I1 232)

Our God, after the storms, will send the calm. (L 233)

Let our soul be sad or glad, in bitterness or joy, at peace or troubled, . . . but all the while the magnet of our heart and mind, our superior will, which is our moral compass, must continually point to the Love of God our Creator, our Saviour, our only Sovereign Good. (I2 324)

Never does our good God leave us save to hold us better; never does He let go of us save to keep us better; never does He wrestle with us save to give Himself up to us and to bless us. (L 38)

God is merciful to those who want to love Him and who have placed their hopes in Him. (L 201–2)

❦

Have Jesus always for your patron, His Cross for a mast on which you must spread your resolutions as a sail. Your anchor shall be a profound confidence in Him, and you shall sail prosperously. (L 75)

God wishes to make all things good and beautiful. (T 54)

By [hope] we accept the promises of good things that we do not see. (T 86)

Man cannot be perfected except by divine goodness.... The one has great need and great capacity to receive good; the other has great abundance and great inclination to bestow it. (T 91)

It behoves us to hope amid trials, and to fear in prosperity, and in both circumstances always to be humble. (I2 343)

Since it is simply the divine essence itself, it is therefore always permanent and eternal. (T 104)

Truly, by the watering of our Savior's blood, made with the hyssop of the cross, we have been restored to a white incomparably better than that possessed by the snows of innocence. (T 115–16)

See, this divine lover is at the gate. He does not merely knock, but he remains there knocking. He calls to the soul. (T 123)

Our divine Savior never forgets to show that "his mercies are above all his works," that his mercy surpasses his justice, ... that his love is infinite. (T 123)

Miraculous graces... have almost in an instant changed wolves into shepherds, rocks into water, and persecutors into preachers.... God in a single instant has raised certain chosen souls from the depths of sin to the heights of grace. (T 131–32)

Hope is a love that expects and aspires. God is that supreme good which hope waits for. (T 145)

By the sacred promises God's goodness has made us our hearts become and remain completely calm. This calm is the root of that most holy virtue which we call hope. (T 144)

We love our fathers, not because they belong to us but rather because we belong to them. It is thus that we love and desire God in hope. (T 147)

There will be nothing which the fullness of his love does not replenish. (T 202)

In the name of the Lord Jesus, how exceeding great are the riches of God's goodness! His love for us is an incomprehensible abyss. Hence he has prepared for us a rich sufficiency, or rather a rich abundance of means proper for our salvation. (T 224)

We must hope that when [temptation] comes God will multiply his graces, redouble his assistance, and give us all needed help, and that while God does not give strength for an imaginary and unnecessary war, he will give it to us when need does arise. (T 231)

The soul that has flowed out into God does not die. How could it die by being plunged into life?... The soul, without losing its own life, no longer lives when mingled with God but rather God lives in it. (T 302)

God always gives His light to those who serve Him. (S3 10)

The greatest defect we have in our prayers and in all that happens to us, particularly in that which concerns tribulations, is our lack of confidence.... Faith is great or little according to the measure of our confidence. (S3 43–44)

Let us walk... joyously, dear souls, among the difficulties of this passing life.... These pains will have an end when our life ends, after which there will be only joy, only contentment, only eternal consolation. (S3 65)

When all shall fail us, then God will take care of us, and then all will not fail us since we shall have God. (S3 120)

God would sooner work miracles than leave without assistance, either spiritual or temporal, those who trust entirely in His Divine Providence. (S3 121)

When human aid fails us, all is not wanting, for God takes over and takes care of us by His special Providence. (S3 121)

Humanity... was actually united to the person of God the Son. For it he destined the incomparable dignity of personal union with his divine majesty, so that it might eternally and pre-eminently enjoy the treasures of his infinite glory. (T 111)

Let us go forward in peace on the way of most holy love, for he who has God's love in death shall possess love eternally after death. (T 225)

He who truly desires Love, seeks it truly. And he who truly seeks it, surely finds it. And he who finds it has found the Fountain of Life. (V 147)

The joys of love surpass the sorrows of death, for death cannot cause those joys to die but heightens them. (T 246)

The Third Glorious Mystery

The Descent of the Holy Spirit

❧

Love of God

[Y]ou shall love the Lord your God with all your heart, and with all your soul, and with all your mind, and with all your strength.—Mark 12:30

The Holy Spirit of God disposes and arranges the devout teaching which He imparts through the lips and pen of His servants with such endless variety, that, although the doctrine is ever one and the same, their treatment of it is different. (I2 v–vi)

Really devout men rise up to God frequently, and with a swift and soaring wing.... Divine Love works in us, and causes us to work briskly and lovingly. (I2 3–4)

The Holy Spirit by the mouths of all the saints and our Lord by His own mouth assure us that a devout life is a life that is sweet, happy, and lovable. (I1 41)

When God intends to perform some act of love in us, by us, and with us, He first suggests it by His inspiration. (I2 107)

Call to mind that God is not only present in the place where you are, but that He is very specially present in your heart and mind, which He kindles and inspires with His Holy Presence, abiding there as Heart of your heart, Spirit of your spirit. (I2 70)

Hatred separates us and love brings us together. The end, then, of love is simply the union of lover and thing loved. (T 75)

If... the real way of attaining to the Love of God is by a careful consideration of all His benefits given to us, then the better we realise these the more we shall love Him. (I2 147)

Were you not summoned by the sweet attractions of the Holy Spirit? Were not the cords by which God drew your little boat to this blessed haven woven out of love and charity? (I1 273)

The whole purpose of preaching the gospel is to set men's hearts on fire. (T 37)

In order to make love of God live and reign within us, let us destroy self-love.... We can at least weaken it in such fashion that even if it lives in us, it does not rule over us. (T 62)

Just as the soul is diffused throughout the entire body and is therefore present in every part of the body but resides in a special manner in the heart, so also God is present in all things but always resides in a special manner in our spirit. (I₁ 85)

As soon as a man gives a little attentive thought to the divinity he feels a certain sweet emotion within his heart, and this testifies that God is God of the human heart. Our mind is never so filled with pleasure as during such thoughts of the divinity. (T 90)

It is not without purpose that this inclination to love God above all things which we possess by nature dwells in our hearts. On God's part, it serves as a crook by which he can gently hold us and draw us to himself. (T 98)

The favoring wind of His most holy inspirations ...comes into our hearts with a gentle force; it seizes them and moves them; it lifts up our thoughts and thrusts our affections into the air of God's love. (T 125)

The Holy Spirit is like a fountain of living water that flows into every part of our hearts so as to spread its grace therein. (T 129)

We are drawn to God not by iron chains, like bulls and buffalos, but by means of allurements, sweet attractions, and holy inspirations. (T 132)

In the same measure as our heart expands itself,...his mercy ever pours forth and increasingly spreads out its holy inspirations. They keep on increasing, and they cause us to increase more and more in sacred love. (T 130)

Imperfect love desires and asks for him; penitence seeks and finds him; perfect love holds and clasps him. (T 155)

If we do not reject the grace of holy love, it goes on expanding with continual increase in souls until they are entirely converted, just as mighty rivers coming upon open plains spread out and ever take up more space. (T 159)

Charity...is a love of friendship.... This preference is incomparable, supreme, and supernatural. It is present in the entire soul like a sun to make it beautiful by its rays. (T 162)

If you love God heartily...you will often speak of Him among your relations, household and familiar friends. (I2 230)

The favorable wind of God's grace fills our soul's canvas.... When our spirit sails along and makes a prosperous voyage, it is not we who cause the wind of inspiration to come to us. (T 216–17)

We neither fill our sails with it nor do we give movement to the ship that is our heart. We merely receive that wind coming from heaven. (T 217)

The heavenly spouse comes into his garden when he comes into a devout soul.... Where can we find better lodging than in the land of the spirit, which he made to his own image and likeness? (T 236)

You cannot imagine what pleasure God takes in hearing the praises that are given Him by the heart that loves Him. He delights exceedingly in the outbursts of our voices and the harmony of our music. (S2 139)

God has placed in our power the acquisition of His pure love which can exalt us infinitely above ourselves. He gives it to whosoever gives Him his. (S2 140)

The more the soul praises, the more it is pleased with praising. (T 255)

If the soul had no love it would never be afflicted with fear that it did not love. (T 308)

Happy we are when we will to love our Lord! Let us, then, love Him well. Let us not set ourselves to consider too exactly what we do for His love, provided we know that we will to do nothing but for His love. (L 35)

Live in such a manner that one will recognize clearly in you a person who loves God with his whole heart, one who keeps the Commandments, frequents the Sacraments, and does all things worthy of a true Christian. (S4 11)

Wherever we may be, provided we have been led there by the Holy Spirit, as Our Lord was led into the desert, we shall have nothing to fear. (S3 29)

We ought not to hesitate to say to God, "I love You," even if we do not have a strong feeling of love, since we wish to love Him and to have an ardent desire of doing so. (S1 27)

If you have the love of God, do not be troubled or anxious about the exercise of the other virtues. For you will not fail to practice them when the opportunity presents itself. (S2 73)

Whoever receives the Holy Spirit is wholly transformed in God. If, then, you wish to know if you have received Him, examine your works, for it is by them that we know the answer. (S2 166)

Sacred love is a miraculous child, since the human will cannot conceive it unless it is infused into our hearts by the Holy Spirit. (T 66)

What could love bring forth that would be unworthy of love and would not tend to love? (T 168)

Our merciful Jesus, who has purchased us with his own blood, infinitely desires us to love him so that we may be saved forever, and he desires us to be saved so that we may love him forever. His love tends to our salvation, and our salvation tends to his love. (T 121)

Charity, which gives life to our hearts, is not extracted from our hearts but is poured into them like a heavenly liquor by the supernatural providence of his divine majesty. (T 161)

Perfection of life is the perfection of love. For love is the life of the soul. (V 21)

We must fear God out of love, not love Him out of fear. (V 22)

The Fourth Glorious Mystery

The Assumption of Mary into Heaven

※

Desire for Heaven

Come, O blessed of my Father, inherit the kingdom prepared for you from the foundation of the world.—Matthew 25:34

Consider the nature God has given to you. It is the highest in this visible world; it is capable of eternal life and of being perfectly united to His Divine Majesty. (I1 53)

Consider the beauty and perfection of the countless inhabitants of that blessed country,—the millions and millions of angels, Cherubim and Seraphim; the glorious company of Apostles, martyrs, confessors, virgins, and saints. (I2 43)

O blessed company, any one single member of which surpasses all the glory of this world, what will it be to behold them all, to sing with them the sweet Song of the Lamb? (I2 43–44)

How good it is to be united forever with the source of all good! (I1 66)

Consider how they enjoy the Presence of God, Who fills them with the richness of His Vision, which is a perfect ocean of delight; the joy of being for ever united to their Head. They are like happy birds, hovering and singing for ever within the atmosphere of divinity, which fills them with inconceivable pleasures. (I2 44)

Let us go forward, my dear soul, to that infinite repose, let us travel on to that blessed land which is promised to us. What are we doing in Egypt? (I1 66)

Behold the Saints, who have left you their example, the millions of holy souls who long after you, desiring earnestly that you may one day be for ever joined to them in their song of praise. (I2 46–47)

The road to Heaven is not so hard to find as the world would have you think. (I2 47)

What should it matter to us whether it is by the desert or by the meadows we go, if God is with us and we go into Paradise? (L 206)

The fulness of joy...is only to be found in Paradise. (I2 134)

❦

Desire for Heaven

You must form clearly in yourself the idea of eternity. Whoever thinks well on this troubles himself little about what happens in these three or four moments of mortal life. (L 156)

The present day is given to you in order to gain the future day of eternity.... Make a firm purpose to employ the day well for this intention. (I1 94)

Can [you] bear to lose your God for ever? (I2 42)

God does not will that our heart should find a place of rest, any more than did the dove that went out from Noah's ark, so that it may return to Himself from whom it came. (I1 282)

Thank God, Who has made you for so gracious an end. (I2 29)

These supernatural affections are chiefly three: the mind's love of the beautiful in the mysteries of faith, its love for the utility of those goods promised us in the life to come, and its love for the supreme goodness of the most holy and eternal God. (T 65)

O holy and unending eternity! Blessed is he who thinks of you. Yes, for what do we play here in this world but a children's game for who knows how many days? It would be nothing whatever, if it were not the passage to eternity. (L 74)

There is an infinite workman who has stamped on me this limitless desire to know and this appetite which cannot be satiated. For this reason I must strive towards him and reach out for him so as to unite and join myself to his goodness. I belong to it and I exist for it. (T 93)

The assurance God gives us that paradise is ours infinitely strengthens our desire to win it. (T 144)

Let us live in peace...and serve God so as to be his in this mortal life and still more so in life eternal. (T 179)

This union our heart aspires to cannot reach perfection in this mortal life. We can begin our love in this life, but we can consummate it only in the life to come. (T 179)

This perfect union of the soul with God will be made only in heaven, where, as the Apocalypse says, "the marriage feast of the Lamb" will be kept. (T 180)

In proportion as you esteem eternal happiness, you will have less fear of leaving this mortal and perishable life. (L 108)

The triumphant love that the blessed put forth in heaven consists in the final, invariable, and everlasting union of the soul with God. (T 186)

What joy there will be for man's heart to look upon God's face, that face so long desired, that face which is the only desire of our souls! Our hearts have a thirst that cannot be quenched by the pleasures of this mortal life. (T 188)

O wonderful but dear unrest of man's heart! O my soul, be ever without rest or tranquillity whatsoever here on this earth, be ever such until at length you have come to the fresh waters of undying life and to God most holy, for they alone can quench your thirst and quiet your desire. (T 189)

In heaven above we shall see and taste all the divinity.... This infinite divinity will always have infinitely greater store of excellences than we can have sufficiency or capacity to receive. (T 199)

Freely and to the full extent of their desires our souls shall swim in the ocean and soar in the air of the divinity. Forever shall they rejoice to see that this air is so unlimited and this ocean so vast that it cannot be measured by their wings. (T 199)

In heaven he will ravish us with the beauty of his wisdom. Then in the abundance of his love he will unveil to us the reasons, means, and motives of all that has taken place in this world to effect our eternal salvation. (T 223)

What joy we shall have in heaven when we behold our hearts' beloved like an infinite sea whose waters are every perfection and goodness!... After so many languors and longings our hearts shall come to that mighty, living fount which is the divinity. (T 234)

Love seeks that which it has already found, not to have it but to have it forever. (T 242)

What contentment will we receive in seeing again those whom we have so dearly loved in this life!... The good friendships of this life will continue eternally in the other. (S3 59)

All our affections will draw their strength from the charity of God which, ordering them all, will make us love each of the blessed with that eternal love with which we are loved by the Divine Majesty. (S3 59)

We will see face to face and very clearly the Divine Majesty, the essence of God, and the mystery of the Most Holy Trinity.... There we will understand and participate in those adorable conversations and divine colloquies which take place between the Father, Son and Holy Spirit. (S3 63)

Consider the nobility and excellence of your soul.... It knows that there is an eternity and knows also what manner is best designed for living well in this visible world so that our soul may be joined with the angels in paradise and enjoy God for all eternity. (I1 282)

Look up to heaven, and do not forfeit it for earth. (I1 291)

The Fifth Glorious Mystery

The Crowning of Mary Queen of Heaven and Earth

Devotion to Mary

Behold, your mother!
—John 19:27

With your inward eyes behold the Blessed Virgin who maternally bids you: "Courage, my child, do not spurn my Son's desires or the many sighs that I have cast forth for you as I yearn with Him for your salvation." (I1 68)

Honor, reverence, and respect with a special love the sacred and glorious Virgin Mary. She is the Mother of our sovereign Father and consequently she is our own Mother in a special way. (I1 106)

Let us run to her and like little children cast ourselves into her arms with perfect confidence. (I1 106)

Rest in peace in the two arms of divine Providence, and in the bosom of the protection of our Lady. (L 106)

First and above all, God destined for his most holy Mother a favor worthy of the love of a Son who, since he is all-wise, all-powerful, and all-good, necessarily prepared a Mother in keeping with himself. (T 116)

Original sin drew back its waters in reverence and awe at the presence of the true tabernacle of the eternal covenant. (T 117)

Like a chosen garden that was to bear the fruit of life, she was made to flower with every kind of perfection. (T 117)

God turned all captivity away from his glorious Mother. To her he gave the blessing of the two states of human nature: she possessed that innocence which the first Adam had lost and she surpassingly enjoyed that redemption which the second Adam gained for her. (T 117)

She is crowned by her own Son, who is the supreme object of love, since children are the crown of their fathers and mothers. (T 118)

All the saints and angels are compared only to the stars, and the first of them to the fairest of the stars, but she is "fair as the moon," and as easily discerned and chosen from among the saints as is the sun from among the stars. (T 183)

She never committed a venial sin, as the Church holds. Hence, for her there was no change or delay in her progress in love but by a perpetual advance she rose from love to love. (T 183)

Since maternal love is the most urgent, the most active, and the most ardent of all forms of love,... how much must it have worked in the heart of such a Mother and for the heart of such a Son? (T 183)

The same nails that crucified the body of that divine Child also crucified the soul of his Mother. The same thorns that pierced his head pierced through the soul of that all-sweet Mother. She felt the same miseries as her Son. (T 244)

[Imitate] the most holy Queen and "Mother of love," whose sacred soul perpetually magnified and exalted God. (T 250)

What can such a Son refuse to the most loving and loved Mother ever? (S4 113)

When was it, I ask you, that our Lord came into his garden except when he came into his Mother's most pure, most humble, and most sweet womb, filled with all the flowering plants of holy virtue? (T 284)

Picture to yourself... the most holy Virgin our Lady when she had conceived the Son of God, her sole love.

The soul of that beloved Mother was completely centered upon that beloved Child. Because the divine loved one was there within her sacred womb. (T 287)

He willed that the most holy Virgin should be the most excellent of all creatures, since He had chosen her from all eternity to be the Mother of His Divine Son. (S4 85)

We must invite her to our banquet too, since where the Son and the Mother are the wine will not fail. (S4 116–17)

If we want Our Lady to ask her Son to change the water of our tepidity into the wine of His love, we must do whatever He tells us. (S4 117)

This sacred Virgin knew that Our Lord, in giving her St. John for a son, was giving her as Mother to all Christians as children of grace, for "John" means grace. (S3 198)

The most sacred Virgin is also that morning star which brings us the gracious news of the coming of the true Sun. (S4 53)

The blows which the blessed body of the Savior received on the Cross caused no wound to the body of Our Lady, but they gave a mighty counter-blow to her soul, so that the prophecy of Simeon was verified. (S2 7)

The sorrows of the Son were the swords which pierced the soul of the Mother.... The thorns, the nails, the lance which pierced the head, the hands, the feet, the side of Our Lord, passed through them to pierce the soul of the Mother. (S2 7)

May our glorious and holiest mistress and queen, the Virgin Mary... present our hearts to her Son and give us His. (L 159)

Who is the child who, if he could, would not raise his good mother and place her in Paradise after her decease? This Mother of God died of love, and the love of her Son resuscitated her. (S2 15–16)

She gave Him a place according to His desire. Now He gives her one according to His love, exalting her above the cherubim and seraphim. (S2 18)

All her perfections, all her virtues, all her happiness are referred, consecrated and dedicated to the glory of her Son, who is their source, their author and finisher. (S2 18)

We call her beautiful, and beautiful far beyond other creatures—but beautiful as the moon, which receives its brightness from that of the sun, for she receives her glory from that of her Son. (S2 20)

If Jesus Christ prays in Heaven, He prays in virtue of Himself; but the Virgin prays only as we do, in virtue of her Son, but with more credit and favor. (S2 21)

In all dangers, in all tempests...look at this star of the sea and invoke her. With her favor your ship will arrive at port without disaster and without shipwreck. (S2 22)

This Virgin asks of you above all, as the most certain demonstration of your devotion to her, that you have her Son for the King of your heart and soul, that He reign in you and that His commandments be carried out. (S2 22)

O God, what honor, love and affection we owe to Our Lady, as much because she is the Mother of our Savior as because she is also ours! (S2 28)

Charity is never idle; it burns in the hearts where it dwells and reigns, and the most blessed Virgin was full of it, because she bore Love Itself in her womb. (S2 50)

Is there any creature to whom the Son of God has said, "My Mother"?... The greatest title that can be given to the Holy Virgin is to name her Mother of God. (S2 107)

What greater happiness could come to a woman than to bear in her womb Him who is equal to the Father—Him whom the heavens cannot contain? (S2 125)

How truly blessed is that womb in which the Son of God has taken human flesh, and what an honor this Virgin has received by giving her most pure blood to form the sacred humanity of the Savior of our souls! (S2 125)

That chaste womb resembles the Ark in which were "the manna, the rod of Aaron which had blossomed, and the tablets of the covenant" of the Law of Moses. What is that manna if not the Son of God who has come down from Heaven? (S2 125–26)

What an honor for us to do battle under this valiant captainess! Women seem to have a particular obligation to follow this courageous warrior, who has so infinitely ennobled and honored them. (S2 148)

If you question her and say: "Mother, what can we do to please you?" no doubt she will answer that she desires and wants you to do what she directed to be done at that celebrated marriage feast of Cana.... If then you listen to her faithfully, you will hear in your heart those very words addressed to you: Do whatever my Son tells you. (S2 196–97)

OTHER TOPICS

Prayer

Watch and pray that you may not enter into temptation.
—Mark 14:38

Perfection does not consist in having these spiritual consolations and affections, but in having our will united to that of God. It is this we may and ought to ask from the Divine Majesty unconditionally. (S1 16)

Retire apart for awhile in order to refresh [yourself], get back [your] breath, and recover strength so that [you] may afterwards more successfully gain ground and advance in the devout life. (I1 35)

Prayer... calls down God's love, and the sacraments confer it. (I1 42)

If possible, [pray] in the morning, which is the best time for spiritual exercises, and think of them during the rest of the day. (I1 52)

[Prayer] is a stream of holy water that flows forth and makes the plants of our good desires grow green and flourish and quenches the passions within our hearts. (I1 81)

I especially counsel you to practice mental prayer, the prayer of the heart, and particularly that which centers on the life and passion of our Lord. (I1 81)

Begin all your prayers, whether mental or vocal, in the presence of God. Keep to this rule without any exception and you will quickly see how helpful it will be. (I1 82)

Do not hurry along and say many things but try to speak from your heart. A single "Our Father" said with feeling has greater value than many said quickly and hurriedly. (I1 82)

The Rosary is a useful devotion when rightly used, and there are various little books to teach this. It is well, too, to say pious Litanies, and other vocal prayers appointed for the Hours and found in Manuals of devotion. (I2 67)

If you have the gift of mental prayer, you should always give it first place. Afterwards if you cannot say your vocal prayers because of your many duties or for some other reason, don't be disturbed on that account. (I1 83)

During vocal prayer if you find your heart drawn and invited to interior or mental prayer, don't refuse to take it up. Let your mind turn very gently in that direction and don't be concerned at not finishing the vocal prayers you intended to say. The mental prayer you substitute for them is more pleasing to God and more profitable for your soul. (I1 83)

It will also be helpful to invoke your guardian angel as well as the holy saints who had a part in the mystery on which you meditate. For example, when meditating on the death of our Lord, you can invoke our Lady, St. John, Mary Magdalen, and the good thief. (I1 86)

Children learn to speak by hearing their mother talk, and stammering forth their childish sounds in imitation; and so if we cleave to the Savior in meditation, listening to His words, watching His actions and intentions, we shall learn in time, through His Grace, to speak, act and will like Himself. (I2 65)

You must even accustom yourself to know how to pass from prayer to all the various duties your vocation and state of life rightly and lawfully require of you, even though they appear far different from the affections you received in prayer. (I1 91)

When your ordinary work or business is not specially engrossing, let your heart be fixed more on God than on it. (I2 175)

If it should happen that you find no joy or comfort in meditation, I urge you not to be disturbed but to open your heart's door to words of vocal prayer. (I1 92)

I should like you to let no day pass without giving half an hour to the reading of some spiritual book, for this would serve as a sermon. (L 45)

Sometimes you can arouse your heart by some act or movement of exterior devotion, such as prostrating yourself on the ground, crossing your hands before your breast, or embracing a crucifix. (I1 92)

Be sure then,...that while externally occupied with business and social duties, you frequently retire within the solitude of your own heart. That solitude need not be in any way hindered by the crowds which surround you—they surround your body, not your soul, and your heart remains alone in the Sole Presence of God. (I2 88)

Our tasks are seldom so important as to keep us from withdrawing our hearts from them from time to time in order to retire into this divine solitude. (I1 97)

By your morning prayer you open your soul's windows to the sunshine of Righteousness. (I2 86)

Make spiritual aspirations to God by short, ardent movements of your heart. Marvel at His beauty, implore His help, cast yourself in spirit at the foot of the cross, adore His goodness. (I1 98)

There is no difficulty in this exercise [prayer of the heart], as it may be interspersed among all our tasks and duties without any inconvenience.... This does not hinder us but rather assists us greatly in what we do. (I1 99)

If the work be such as to require your undivided attention, then pause from time to time and look to God, even as navigators who make for the haven they would attain, by looking up at the heavens rather than down upon the deeps on which they sail. So doing, God will work with you, in you, and for you, and your work will be blessed. (I2 176)

You should remain for some time alone with yourself in your room or garden or some other place. There you will have leisure to withdraw your spirit into your heart and refresh your soul with pious meditations, holy thoughts, or a little spiritual reading. (I1 191)

Among all these tasks mingle reflections. (I1 215)

We retire with God, because we aspire to Him, and we aspire in order to retire with Him; so that aspiration after God and spiritual retreat excite one another, while both spring from the one Source of all holy thoughts. (I2 90)

Prayer is a colloquy, a discussion, or a conversation of the soul with God. (T 268)

Meditation is similar to one who smells a pink, rose, rosemary, thyme, hyacinth, and orange blossom separately one after the other. Contemplation is like one who smells water containing perfume made up of all those flowers. (T 280–81)

When we think upon the things of God, not to learn but rather to acquire affection for them, the act is called meditating and the exercise is meditation. (T 272)

Meditation is the mother of love but contemplation is its daughter. (T 276)

Ordinarily, to attain to contemplation we must hear Sacred Scripture, ... read devout books, pray, meditate, sing canticles, and think good thoughts. Hence, since holy contemplation is the end and aim to which all these exercises tend, they are all reduced to it. (T 285)

Those wishing to pray place themselves in God's presence by retiring within themselves and as it were bringing their soul into their heart to speak there with God. Such recollection is made by the command of love, which arouses us to pray and causes us to take this means to pray well. Hence we ourselves make this withdrawal of our spirit. (T 286)

Remain in peace, in repose, in quiet, close to Jesus, [your] gentle Master. (T 291)

[The] will ... to be in prayer without any aim but to be in God's sight as it shall please him, is a supremely excellent quiet. It is such because it is pure and free from any kind of self-interest. (T 299)

It is a very good prayer simply to present one's needs to Our Lord, place them before the eyes of His goodness, and leave it to Him to act as He sees fit, convinced that He will answer us according to our needs. (S4 110)

Certainly one can pray not only for spiritual, but for temporal things as well. That can and ought to be done, since Our Lord Himself taught us to do so. (S4 110-11)

What is prayer and meditation? It seems that these words have come from another planet since so few people want to understand them.... To make prayer is to pray. To pray with attention is to have a lively, vigilant, attentive faith. (S3 43)

We learn [prayer] more by experience than by being taught. (S1 1)

All people can pray.... No one can excuse himself from doing so. (S1 8)

How necessary prayer is for man, since if a tree does not have sufficient earth to cover its roots it cannot live; neither can a man live who does not give special attention to heavenly things. (S1 5)

Prayer is a sovereign remedy, it lifts the mind to God. (I2 320)

We pray in order to speak with God, and to hear Him speak to us by inspirations and movements in the interior of our soul. (L 27)

Those who pray with perfection ask for very few [temporal] goods, remaining rather before God like children before their father, placing in Him all their confidence. (S1 17)

The Our Father and the Creed we ought to recite every day. (S1 18)

To mutter something with the lips is not praying if one's heart is not joined to it.... Prayer is nothing other than speaking to God. (S1 18)

Prayer is nothing else but an elevation of our mind to God.... When we have our Savior in our arms everything becomes easy for us. (S2 94)

You tell me that you do not have the time to give two or three hours to prayer. Who asks you to do so?... Who can prevent you from speaking to Him in the depth of your heart, since it makes no difference whether you speak to Him mentally or vocally? Make short but fervent aspirations. (S1 26–27)

The Eucharist

He who eats my flesh and drinks my blood has eternal life, and I will raise him up at the last day.—John 6:54

By Holy Communion [the soul] gives herself up to her Savior and happily enters into His holy love. (I1 35)

It is not without purpose that our Savior calls Himself "the bread that came down from heaven." (I1 82)

Whosoever receives [Communion] frequently and devoutly, so strengthens the health and life of his soul, that it is hardly possible for him to be poisoned by any evil desires. (I2 116)

[You] can avoid spiritual death by virtue of this sacrament of life. (I1 115)

There is nothing in the married life to hinder frequent Communion. Most certainly the Christians of the Primitive Church communicated daily, whether married or single. (I2 119)

Frequent Communion is by no means inconsistent with the state of parents, husbands, and wives, provided the person who communicates is prudent and discreet. (I1 117)

Have a great desire to communicate. (I1 117)

Go with great confidence and with great humility to receive this heavenly food which nourishes you for everlasting life. (I1 117)

When you have received [Communion]...adore the King of our Salvation, tell Him of all your own personal matters, and realise that He is within you, seeking your best happiness. (I2 121)

The Saviour instituted the most holy Sacrament of the Eucharist, really containing His Body and His Blood, in order that they who eat it might live for ever. (I2 116)

Your main intention in Communion should be to grow, strengthen, and abound in the Love of God; for Love's Sake receive that which Love Alone gives you. (I2 121)

You cannot consider our Savior in an action more full of love or more tender than this. In it He abases Himself, and changes Himself into food, so that He may penetrate our souls and unite Himself most intimately to the heart and body of His faithful. (I1 118)

You receive Communion...to learn to love God, be purified from your imperfections, delivered from misery, comforted in affliction, and supported in weakness. (I1 118)

Communicate with your Perfection, your Strength, your Physician. (I2 122)

The strong [need Communion] lest they become weak, and the weak that they may become strong; the sick that they may be restored to health, and the healthy lest they fall sick. (I1 118–19)

Go often to Communion, as often as you can. (I1 119)

Those who do not have many worldly affairs to look after ought to communicate often because they have leisure to do so and those who have great undertakings because they have need to do so, since one who labors hard and is weighed down with troubles should eat solid food and do so frequently. (I1 119)

You receive the Blessed Sacrament often so as to learn how to receive it well, for we hardly do an action well which we do not practice often. (I1 119)

Adoring and feeding upon Beauty, Goodness, and Purity itself in this most Divine Sacrament you too will become lovely, holy, pure. (I2 123)

Infinite happiness... has not only been promised to us but we have a pledge of it in the most holy sacrament of the Eucharist, the perpetual feast of divine grace. (T 191)

It is impossible to state how much the Savior desires to enter into our souls. (T 248)

[The Eucharist] is given into our own bodily mouths so that we may know that he will give us his own divine essence in an eternal feast of glory. (T 191–92)

[Faithful communicants] know that their Savior in body and soul is present with a most real presence in their body and their soul in this most adorable sacrament. (T 288)

The divine sacrament... contains the dew of all heavenly blessings. (T 288)

[Faithful communicants] adore this sovereign king newly present in their inmost being with his awesome presence... for the unbelievable spiritual consolation and refreshment they receive in knowing by faith this divine seed of immortality within themselves. (T 288)

How wonderful to be nourished on the Bread come down from Heaven, the Bread of angels! It is even more wonderful by the love with which It is given by Him who is at once both Gift and Giver. (S4 56)

Between the mystery of the Eucharist and that of the Incarnation there is only one difference: in the Incarnation we see the incarnate God in His own Person, and in the Eucharist we see Him under a more hidden and obscure form. In both instances it is the same God-man who was born of the Virgin. (S4 69–70)

Consolation comes to us from our faith in the Eucharist. (S4 105)

The Precious Blood of Our Lord... expels the venom of sin, which is poisonous to our souls. By the Sacrament of the Eucharist, the fruit of our Redemption is applied to us. (S4 116)

He bestowed on us the means to reach the supreme degree of union which He desired for us, namely, to be made one with Him as He and His Father are One, that is, one same reality. (S3 95)

Note that the first miracle was wrought by changing water into wine, just as the last wrought by Jesus Christ in His mortal sojourn was the changing of wine into His Blood in the Most Holy Sacrament of the Eucharist. (S4 105)

Those early Christians had so fervent a love for each other that their wills and their hearts were all holily blended as one.... What built that great union among them was none other, my dear souls, than the most Holy Communion. (S3 89)

What divine fragrance He spread before the Divine Majesty when He instituted the Most Holy Sacrament of the Altar, where He so admirably demonstrated to us the greatness of His love. (S3 95)

Keep carefully to frequent Communion: believe me, you could do nothing more certain to strengthen yourself in virtue. (L 70)

Confession

Receive the Holy Spirit. If you forgive the sins of any, they are forgiven; if you retain the sins of any, they are retained.
—John 20:22–23

The first purgation we must make is that of sin and the way to make it is by the holy sacrament of penance. (I1 49)

Look for the best confessor you can, and then get some of the little books written to help our conscience make a good confession. (I1 49)

Proceed with a humble and confident mind to make your general confession. Don't let fears of any sort disturb you. (I1 71)

When you kneel before your spiritual director, imagine that you are on Mount Calvary at the feet of Jesus Christ crucified and that His Precious Blood drops down on every side to cleanse away your iniquities. (I1 71)

Put away your sins by confessing them, for in proportion as they are put out, so will the Precious Merits of the Passion of Christ come in and fill you with blessings.
(I2 52)

In His sacrament He will put Himself as a seal and sacred signet upon your heart, now made new again. In this way, your soul will be purged from sin and from all affection for sin. (I1 74–75)

Never let your soul remain long infected by sin since you have a remedy so near at hand and so easy to apply. (I1 111)

Be sure to state everything with candor and sincerity and in this way put your conscience completely at rest. This done, listen to the advice and commands of God's minister and say within your heart, "Speak, Lord, for your servant hears." (I1 71–72)

Hear in spirit the words of absolution which the same Savior of your soul, seated on the throne of His mercy on high in heaven will pronounce before all the angels and saints at the same instant as the priest in His name absolves you here below on earth. (I1 74)

Our Savior gave the sacrament of penance and confession to His Church so that we may be cleansed from all our iniquities no matter how often and how greatly we have been defiled by them. (I1 111)

As to confession, I advise you to frequent it even more, especially if you fall into some imperfection by which your conscience is troubled. (L 44)

In confession you not only receive absolution from the venial sins you confess but also great strength to avoid them in the future, light to see them clearly, and abundant grace to repair whatever damage you have incurred. (I1 111–12)

You will also practice the virtues of humility, obedience, simplicity, and charity. In the single act of confession you will exercise more virtues than in any other act whatsoever. (I1 112)

Many who confess their venial sins out of custom and concern for order but without thought of amendment remain burdened with them for their whole life and thus lose many spiritual benefits and advantages. (I1 112)

It is an abuse to confess any kind of sin, whether mortal or venial, without a will to be rid of it since confession was instituted for no other purpose. (I1 112)

Don't be satisfied with confessing your venial sins merely as to the fact but accuse yourself of the motive that led you to commit them. (I1 113)

Go to your confessor, open your heart thoroughly, let him see every corner of your soul, and take all his advice with the utmost simplicity and humility.... [God] often makes the counsel we take, specially that of the guides of souls, to be more useful than would seem likely. (I2 336)

After [a devout person] has re-examined his heart in order to renovate it, he must anoint it with the sacraments of confession and Holy Eucharist. Such an exercise will restore your strength...warm up your heart, bring new life to your good resolutions, and make your soul's virtues flourish with fresh vigor. (I1 272)

There is no sin, however great and grievous it may be, which cannot be pardoned in this life, if one confesses it. This is an article of faith. (S3 81)

What does it cost us to hear the words, "I absolve you of all your sins," or to receive the Most Holy Sacrament in which is contained all heavenly and earthly delights? (S2 43)

The Mass

A man once gave a great banquet.
—Luke 14:16

The sun of all spiritual exercises [is] the most holy, sacred, and supremely sovereign sacrament and sacrifice of the Mass. (I1 103)

The Mass [is] the center of the Christian religion, heart of devotion, and soul of piety. (I1 103)

[The Mass is] the ineffable mystery that comprises within itself the deepest depths of divine charity, the mystery in which God really gives Himself and gloriously communicates His graces and favors to us. (I1 103)

Prayer made in union with this divine sacrifice has inestimable power, so that by it the soul overflows with heavenly favors as if "leaning on her Beloved." (I1 103)

The choirs of the Church triumphant and those of the Church militant are united to our Lord in this divine action, so that with Him, in Him, and through Him they may ravish the heart of God the Father and make His mercy all our own. (I1 104)

If some strict duty keeps you from being present in person at the celebration of this sovereign sacrifice, try at least to transport your heart to it and assist at Mass by your spiritual presence. (I1 104)

At the Last Supper...He had given the incomparable pledge of His love for us men, the Most Blessed Sacrament of the Eucharist. (S3 85)

Sometime during the morning go in spirit into the church, if you cannot do so otherwise, unite your intention with that of all Christians,...make the same interior acts that you would make if you were really present in church at the offering of Holy Mass. (I1 104)

Fix your heart on the mysteries of the Word, and unite yourself to the Death and Passion of our Redeemer, now actually and essentially set forth in this holy Sacrifice, which, together with the priest and all the congregation, you offer to God the Father, to His Glory and your own salvation. (I2 100)

From the communion to the end of Mass give thanks to Jesus Christ for His incarnation, life, passion, and death, and for the love He manifests in this Holy Sacrifice. Implore Him always to be merciful to you, your parents, friends, and the whole Church. (I1 105)

When you cannot enjoy the benefit of communicating in reality at Holy Mass, go to Communion at least in heart and spirit by uniting yourself in ardent desire to the life-giving Body of the Savior. (I1 118)

Remember, it is His Majesty who speaks to us and makes known His will. Thus, with a spirit of devotion and attention, let us hear the truths which the preacher proposes to us. (S3 157)

In public prayer we ought to be particularly attentive on account of the edification of our neighbor; exterior reverence is a great aid to the interior. (S1 22)

The Church

So now I say to you: You are Peter and on this rock I will build my Church. And the gates of the underworld can never hold out against it.—Matthew 16:18

Always and with all my heart, I submit my writings, my words, and my actions to the correction of the most holy, catholic, apostolic, and Roman Church. (T 49)

You are a daughter of the Church, and rejoice in this. For the children of this mother who are willing to live according to her laws always die happily.... It is a great consolation at death to have been a child of Holy Church. (L 109)

The truths of the Faith are sometimes agreeable to the human spirit, not only because God has revealed them by His word and proposed them by His Church, but also because these truths suit our taste.... They are according to our inclinations. (L 21)

Before all it is necessary to keep the general commandments of God and the Church, which are made for every faithful Christian. Without this there can be no devotion in the world. (L 7)

The Church

Use diligently all the Church's means to save yourself and to love God. Yes, O my God, I will be assiduous in prayer and at the sacraments. I will listen to His holy Word and put Your inspirations and counsels into practice. (I1 57)

The Church is adorned with a surpassing variety of instructive books, sermons, treatises, and devotional works, each one of them most beautiful and pleasing to the sight. (T 37–38)

In the doctrine the Church puts forth we find the fine gold of holy charity.... It gilds all the science of the saints and raises it above every other science. (T 38)

In holy Church all is by love, in love, for love, and of love. (T 38)

God is more glorified when we unite with our brethren and neighbours and join our offerings to theirs. (I2 102)

I know that [the Church] is "the pillar and ground of truth," in which she can neither deceive nor be deceived. (T 49–50)

[Come] to the school of wisdom. (T 127)

The Holy Spirit... invisibly presides over councils and has judged, determined, and concluded the matter by the mouth of his servants whom he has established as the pastors of Christendom. (T 140)

It is this holy passion which causes so many books of devotion to be written, so many churches, altars, and religious houses to be built.... It is this passion that makes so many of God's servants watch, labor, and die amid those flames of zeal which consume and devour them. (T 258)

Holy Church usually prepares us for great solemnities with vigils to help us appreciate more the great benefits we have received from God in the events celebrated. (S4 50)

In this present life we bear the name of Christ, namely "Christians", and we are anointed by the Sacraments which we receive. (S4 100)

Everyone must believe all the truths of faith—both those which God Himself has directly revealed, as well as those He has revealed through His Church. (S3 35)

That naked and simple faith is that by which we believe the truths of the Faith...solely by the acquiescence of our spirit in the authority of the word of God and the proposition of the Church. (L 22)

All the truths necessary for salvation...are revealed by God and made known by the Church. (S3 39)

The Church

Although the Apostles died, the College of Apostles did not die.... The College of Apostles has passed down to us and will last until the end of the world. (S3 79)

Our Lord chose St. Peter to be the head of all His priests. (S3 100)

All Christians share in all the prayers and good works which are offered in Holy Mother Church. This communion exists not only here below on earth, but in Heaven as well. (S3 101)

The Church is the house of the Father of the family, who is our Lord and Master; He takes very great care to provide for the necessities of all the faithful who are associated there. (S3 119–20)

We have the Sacraments of Holy Church to wash us from our iniquities, for they are like channels through which the merits of the Savior's Passion flow into us so that through them we recover grace when we have lost it. (S3 142)

Monks and nuns have voluntarily enclosed themselves in monasteries that they may chant the praise of their God. So their principal exercise ought to be prayer and obedience to that saying which Our Lord gives in the Gospel: "Pray always." (S1 4)

Our Fathers or rosaries are prescribed for the gaining of indulgences. If we omit saying these, we do not sin, but our good Mother the Church, to show us that she wishes us to say them, grants indulgences to those who do recite them. (S1 19)

All the ceremonies of the Church are full of very great mysteries, and humble, simple, devout people find the greatest consolation in assisting at them. (S1 22)

Tradition and the Church... are infallible witnesses. (S2 5)

We who are Christians believe, assert, and preach because Tradition supports it, because the Church bears witness to it. (S2 14)

Every year Holy Church commemorates the principal actions of our Divine Savior, of Our Lady and Mistress, and of many of the saints whom she presents to us as patrons to imitate. (S2 38)

Holy Church, like a wise mother, from time to time throughout the year gives us special feasts in order to encourage us to renew our good purposes. (S2 81)

All Christians are these princes and knights who dwell in the court of this Sovereign King Our Lord, which is nothing else but the Church. Our dear Savior looks at them all. (S2 128)

Besides the favors which He bestows on all the children of His Church, there are particular ones for those whom

He withdraws into His cabinet, that is to say, into religion. (S2 128)

We must understand the holy and sacred Name of Jesus which means Savior, by which He came to save the world. It is the Name which has remained engraved in His Church and in the heart of every one of its true children. (S2 128)

The Apostles' Creed is so called because it was composed by the Apostles. In it is contained all that we are obliged to believe—if not in detail, at least in general. (S2 191)

Marriage and Family Life

🌿

Every sound tree bears good fruit, but the bad tree bears evil fruit.—Matthew 7:17

Devout souls wed care of the exterior house to that of the interior, that is, the love of their earthly spouse with that of the heavenly Spouse. (I1 70)

In marriage there is communication of life, work, goods, affection, and indissoluble fidelity and therefore married friendship is true, holy friendship. (I1 170)

[Marriage] is honorable to all persons, in all persons, and in all things, that is, in all its parts. (I1 219)

Marriage is a great Sacrament both in Jesus Christ and His Church, and one to be honoured to all, by all and in all. To all, for even those who do not enter upon it should honour it in all humility. (I2 270)

[Marriage] is the nursery of Christianity, which supplies the earth with faithful souls to fill up the number of the elect in heaven. (I1 219–20)

The preservation of holy marriage is of the highest importance for the state since it is the origin and source of all that flows from the state. (I1 220)

Would to God that His well-beloved Son were invited to every marriage, as He was to the marriage at Cana, for then the wine of His consolation and blessing would never be lacking to it. (I1 220)

He who would find a blessing in his marriage, must ponder the holiness and dignity of this Sacrament. (I2 271)

With the great apostle I say to you, "Husbands, love your wives as Christ also loved the Church," and you wives, love your husbands as the Church loves her Savior. (I1 220)

It is God's Invisible Hand Which binds you in the sacred bonds of marriage; it is He Who gives you one to the other, therefore cherish one another with a holy, sacred, heavenly love. The first effect of this love is the indissoluble union of your hearts. (I2 272)

A father's gentle, loving rebuke has far greater power to correct a child than rage and passion. (I1 150)

This union must be understood principally not of the body but of the heart, affections, and love. (I1 221)

[Another] fruit of marriage is the birth and lawful rearing of children. It is a great honor to you who are married that in God's design to multiply souls who can bless and praise Him for all eternity He empowers you to cooperate with Him in so noble a work. (II 221)

Husbands, preserve a tender, constant, heartfelt love for your wives. The woman was taken from the first man on the side nearest his heart so that she might be heartily and tenderly loved by him. (II 221)

Wives, love the husbands God has given you with a love that is tender and heartfelt and yet filled with respect and reverence. (II 221)

He has willed that woman should depend on man, since she is bone of his bone and flesh of his flesh, and that she should be made of a rib taken from beneath his arm to show that she must be under her husband's hand and guidance. All Holy Scripture explicitly enjoins such submission. (II 222)

Perfection of friendship presupposes sure trust in the virtue of those we love. (II 222)

If you married men wish your wives to be faithful to you, teach them by your example.... Do you want them to be chaste? Then conduct yourselves chastely toward them. (II 222)

Wives, your honor is inseparably joined to modesty and purity. Be zealous therefore to preserve your glory and do not permit loose conduct of any sort to tarnish your spotless reputation. (I1 223)

Before giving birth to S. Augustine, S. Monica offered him repeatedly to God's Glory, as he himself tells us; and it is a good lesson for Christian women how to offer the fruit of their womb to God, Who accepts the free oblations of loving hearts, and promotes the desires of such faithful mothers. (I2 277)

[Love children] with a reverential love, as a sacred deposit from God. (I2 277)

When children grow up and begin to have the use of reason both their fathers and their mothers must most carefully impress the fear of God on their hearts. (I1 224)

Raising a house, that is, a family, does not consist in building a splendid residence and storing up vast worldly possessions but in training children well in the fear of God and in virtue. No trouble or labor should be spared to do this, for children are their father's and mother's crown. (I1 224–25)

Wives should desire that their husbands be kept with the sugar of devotion. Without devotion a man is a severe, harsh, rough creature and without devotion a woman is very frail and apt to decline in virtue or lose it. (I1 225)

The Holy Spirit [cannot] remain in a home where there are quarrels, recriminations, and the echoing sounds of scolding and strife. (I1 226)

[Husbands and wives] should recover breath in our Lord to support the burdens of their vocation. (I1 226)

Everybody fulfils his special calling better when subject to the influence of devotion:—family duties are lighter, married love truer, ... every kind of occupation more acceptable and better performed where that is the guide. (I2 10)

The roof under which a good woman dwells is as holy as a church. (SFS 97)

Sexual intercourse does not cease to be a virtuous and holy act, provided the rule of generation is followed. No accidental condition whatsoever can change the law that the principal end of marriage has imposed. (I1 228)

Cross the threshold of marriage hand in hand with courage and confidence, with faith and hope, and with a love that makes all things bearable. (SFS 96)

The love of husband and wife must be sweet, peaceful, firm, and steady and it must be so principally because

God orders and wills it. I say the same about love for our children, near relatives, and friends. (I1 279)

Let married people remain on their cross of obedience, which is in marriage. It is the best and most practical cross for them and one of the most demanding, in that there is almost continual activity—and occasions for suffering are more frequent in this state than in any other. (S3 203)

The angels of little children love with a special love those who bring up children in the fear of God, and who instill into their tender hearts true devotion. (L 227)

The state of marriage is one that requires more virtue and constancy than any other: it is a perpetual exercise of mortification. (V 100)

He has left you precious pledges of your marriage. Keep your eyes to look after their bringing up; keep your mind to raise up theirs. (L 130)

My dear daughter, the child who is taking shape in your womb will be a living image of the divine majesty. (L 86)

There is certainly no doubt that persons may aspire and attain to perfection by remaining in the world and doing carefully what pertains to their vocation. (S3 118)

The Priesthood

🌱

"As the Father has sent me, even so I send you." And when he had said this, he breathed on them, and said to them, "Receive the Holy Spirit."—John 20:21

Devoutly receive the blessing which our Dear Lord gives you through the channel of His minister. (I2 100)

Nothing more difficult nor more dangerous can happen to a man than to hold in his hands and bring to be, through his words, Him whom the angels, so far beyond our conception and praise, cannot comprehend or sufficiently extol. (SFS 46)

We can never preach too much...for heresy is kept alive by preaching and can be defeated only by preaching. (SFS 48)

If every day men brave the storms and perils of the sea attracted by the hope of earthly gain, should the ministers of Jesus Christ, whose aims are incomparably higher, be cowardly enough to hold back because of risks and obstacles? (SFS 56)

God deprived me of myself to make me His and to give me to my people. (SFS 88)

One must adapt oneself.... I have no scruple in departing from my regulation in the service of my flock.
(SFS 90–91)

Priests, bishops and religious... are more especially dedicated to Our Lord. (S4 91)

Priests, being completely dedicated to God, should have no other lord but Him. That is why they detach themselves from the creature by renouncing marriage, the better to unite themselves more intimately to their God. (S3 101)

The Bible

🌿

Heaven and earth will pass away, but my words will not pass away.—Matthew 24:6

It is a good and profitable sign when we take pleasure in hearing God's Word. (I2 108)

It is by listening to preaching that we receive good inspirations and pass from sin to grace. It is by good reading, too, that the heart comes alive and ever gains new strength and vigor. (S4 13)

In many places in Holy Scripture God recommends to us fidelity in following good impulses, lights and inspirations. In such the greatness of His mercy surely shines forth. (S4 42)

By using the words of Holy Scripture our dear Master overcame all the temptations the enemy presented to Him. (S3 18–19)

In our attempt to draw different meanings from Scripture, we must never go beyond legitimate bounds in proposing our interpretations. (S3 103)

We ought never to reject God's word or the teachings Our Lord has left us because of the faults of preachers who propose them. Since our Divine Master pronounced them first with His divine mouth, we are inexcusable if we do not receive them. (S3 158)

Be devoted to the word of God whether you hear it in familiar conversation with spiritual friends or in sermons. Always listen to it with attention and reverence. (I1 107)

Cultivate a special devotion to God's Word, whether studied privately or in public; always listen to it with attention and reverence, strive to profit by it, and do not let it fall to the ground, but receive it within your heart as a precious balm. (I2 105)

The Word of God is pure, and it will make those pure who study it. (I2 184)

The Saints

🍓

The virtuous will shine like the sun in the kingdom of their Father.—Matthew 13:43

Accept the help that the Virgin and the saints offer you. Promise that you will press forward on your way to join them. (I₁ 68)

Pray for the Church, our pastors, relatives, friends, and others, using for that purpose the intercession of our Lady, the angels, and the saints. (I₁ 89)

Implore the intercession of the Virgin and the saints.
(I₁ 58)

The holy souls of the dead who dwell in paradise with the angels...also perform this office of inspiring us and interceding for us by their holy prayers....Let us join our hearts to these heavenly spirits and blessed souls. (I₁ 106)

Just as young nightingales learn to sing in company with the old, so also by our holy associations with the saints let us learn the best way to pray and sing God's praise.
(I₁ 106)

The Saints

Choose certain particular saints whose lives you can best appreciate and imitate and in whose intercession you may have particular confidence. The saint whose name you bear was already assigned to you at baptism. (I1 107)

You should also read stories and lives of the saints for there, as in a mirror, you can see a picture of the Christian life and adapt their deeds to your use in keeping with your vocation. (I1 108)

It is quite evident that the saints and the people who are in Paradise do pray, since they are with the angels who pray. (S1 8)

Acts of the saints cannot be strictly imitated by people living in the world, yet they can be followed either closely or from a distance. (I1 108)

Let us feed on honey found in the works of instruction that devout persons of ancient days have left us. (I1 238)

With respect to Our Lady, the Saints, and your Guardian Angel—do you love them well? Do you rejoice in the sense of their guardianship? Do you take pleasure in their lives, their pictures, their memories? (I2 356)

Look at the example given by saints in every walk of life. There is nothing that they have not done in order to love God and be His devoted followers. (I1 284)

I would wish you to consider how many saints have been in your vocation and state, and how they have accommodated themselves to it with great sweetness and resignation, both under the New and the Old Testaments.... Let this encourage you, recommending yourself to their prayers. (L 12)

In heaven... the loving attention of the blessed is firm, constant, and inviolable and can neither perish nor decrease. (T 181)

Even though some of our feasts are dedicated to the saints, all are consecrated to Our Lord, who made them and to whom they all belong. (S4 88)

On All Saints Day... Holy Church represents to us the glory and felicity of the blessed, for which we long and in which we hope. (S2 81)

In the heavenly Jerusalem, then, we will enjoy a very pleasing conversation with the blessed spirits, the angels, the cherubim and seraphim, the saints, with our Lady and glorious Mistress, with Our Lord and with the thrice holy and adorable Trinity—a conversation which will last forever and will be perpetually cheerful and joyous. (S3 64)

The Virgin and the saints are mediators of grace. They pray for us that we may be pardoned—all through the mediation of the Passion of the Savior. They entrust themselves to the Savior for this. (S2 21)

Although in going to God we meet the angels or the saints on our way, we do not raise our mind to them nor do we address our prayers to them.... We simply ask them to join their prayers to ours in order to make of them a holy fusion, so that by this sacred mingling ours might be better received by the Divine Goodness. (S2 94)

The Savior... willed and ordained that we have recourse to the invocation of the saints. He has granted great favors to people through their intercession, and at other times He has employed that of the angels. (S2 167)

We must avail ourselves of [the saints'] assistance in what benefits us for eternity, beseeching them to obtain the grace of God and the virtues for us, employing the credit they have with our dear Savior and Master. (S2 168)

The Angels

🌿

I tell you that their angels in heaven are continually in the presence of my Father in heaven.—Matthew 18:11

With all his power your guardian angel also urges you to [choose heaven] and in God's name offers you a thousand graces and a thousand helps to assist you to obtain it. (I1 67)

Reach out your hand to your guardian angel so that he may lead you on. Encourage your soul to make this choice. (I1 68)

Since God often sends us inspirations by means of His angels, we should frequently return our aspirations to Him by the same messengers. (I1 106)

Have a particular love and reverence both for the guardian angel of the diocese where you live and those of the persons with whom you live, and especially for your own guardian angel. (I1 107)

Seek to be familiar with the Angels; learn to realise that they are continually present, although invisible. (I2 104)

Pray often to them... and use their aid and assistance in all your affairs, both spiritual and temporal, so that they may cooperate with your intentions. (I1 107)

The angels have care for our salvation and are diligent to procure it, yet they are not solicitous, worried, and anxious. (I1 151)

In the angelic nature he arranged the various hierarchies and orders of which Scripture and the sacred doctors have taught us. (T 108)

There are just as many different graces as there are angels. (T 119)

Our guardian angels foresee goods that are due to us and in this way give us a foretaste of them. So too, in contrary fashion, they arouse in us certain fears and terrors amid unknown dangers so that we may call upon God and remain on guard. (T 142)

I salute the guardian angel of each one of my audience and I beg him to make the heart under his care ready for my words. Very great favors have come to me by this means. (S3 xxi)

[In Heaven] our good angels will give us greater joy than we can imagine when we recognize them and they speak to us so lovingly of the care they had for our salvation during our mortal life, reminding us of the holy inspirations they gave us, as a sacred milk which they drew from the breast of the Divine Goodness. (S3 59)